A PEOPLE PREPARED

The Methodist Way in Faith,
History and Practice

This book was bought by me at Wydale Hall where a Retreat was held for N. Hull Circuit and conducted by the Author. He is a real servant of God and helped me to have a memorable week-end

July 62

JOHN BANKS

A PEOPLE PREPARED

The Methodist Way
in Faith, History and Practice

LONDON
THE EPWORTH PRESS

FIRST PUBLISHED IN 1961

© THE EPWORTH PRESS 1961

Book Steward
FRANK H. CUMBERS

SET IN MONOTYPE BASKERVILLE AND PRINTED IN GREAT BRITAIN BY THE CAMELOT PRESS LTD LONDON AND SOUTHAMPTON

Our conquering Lord
Hath prospered His word,
Hath made it prevail,
And mightily shaken the kingdom of hell.
His arm He hath bared,
And a people prepared
His glory to show,
And witness the power of His passion below.

Dedicated to
ERIC PEDLEY
ERIC KENT
REGINALD SHAW
LEAH CLINTON
RUSSELL LUCKOCK
KATHLEEN FRANKLIN
HEATHER HOMER
PETER ASHCROFT
MARGARET BANKS

the first inheritors of this book, who
created the House Fellowships at Great Barr

Contents

Preface

IN 1759 John Wesley visited Norwich and met the Society at five in the morning. He found there five hundred members, but added: 'A hundred and fifty of these do not *pretend* to meet (in class) at all. Of those, therefore, I make no account. They hang on but a single thread.' What account would he make of modern Methodism where for the large majority the class-meeting is 'of blessed memory'? He would no doubt add his own pungent comment to the funeral notes of our friends who, like Canon Wickham, have written of the class-meeting like this: Wesley 'forged a chain of steel, flexible yet each link with its own strength, and the "glorious failure" of Methodism may not be entirely unrelated to the gradual neglect of his premises in the palmy days of the great congregations.'

Yet today, I believe, we have the chance to recover this most vital 'chain of steel'. Indeed, under the mercy and judgement of God, the times drive us to it. The dispersion of our members to new sparsely churched housing-estates should encourage Christians to use their homes as centres of fellowship; the fact that those housing-estates lack any communal sense should give a great impetus to such small warm-hearted fellowships where a man may feel he is wanted, and not just one of those who catch the 8.15 in the morning. There is a lack of Church attendance today, but there is also a great discussing of the faith which such groups can build upon. It looks, too, as if we may have time in the future to return to these our first works: is not television entertainment killing the Church concert, and the multiple store out-bargaining the Church bazaar (thank God)? God may be throwing us back to finding money for the Church by that earliest and best method —Christian Stewardship. Men ask: 'How shall we fill the gap thus created?' 'Go to, let us have a class-meeting,' they say.

This is just the point where we discover that it is not as easy as it sounds, and we should be warned lest we give up trying too soon. We Methodists have lost the art of class-meetings, and with it much of our lay leadership and many candidates for the Ministry. But it is the belief of this book that the situation is recoverable, and two years of experiment have shown that, given two things, class-meetings can be created. These two things are—

First, the willingness of laymen to accept training and discipline in spiritual leadership. Those who first used this book met as often as possible before each fortnightly 'House Fellowship' to discuss their work with the ministers.

Second, the willingness of those leaders to gather a group around them by persistent, careful and regular visitation of those committed to their charge. This is hard work and seems at first like trying to move a glacier, but often, when members refuse to meet, non-members and even non-Christians are eager to do so and the class becomes a lively mission field.

The chapters of this book were written both to help such a group of lay leaders to do these things in a Methodist Circuit, and to provide material for them to use in their fellowship and background reading from the Bible and the *Methodist Hymn-book* as well as questions for discussion and a prayer to bring the meeting to a close. It is hoped that others will find them helpful as they engage in the same work, so that we may rediscover the height and depth of our inheritance and become *a people prepared* for the task God has given us.

LEEDS
St Andrew's Day 1960

JOHN BANKS

ONE

Belief in God

IT IS AN astounding thing that for the Christian the Cross reveals God's love. Yet it also demonstrates all the things which make it difficult for some men to believe; here was pain, injustice, inhumanity, good seemingly defeated—what John Keats called 'the giant agony of the world'. Here was, by all standards, a good man, and they flogged Him, spat on Him, crucified Him and sat down to watch Him die. 'How can *that* reveal God?' men say. 'If men are allowed to die like that, where is God?' The writer of Psalm 42 knew the question, but not the answer—'As with a sword in my bones, mine adversaries reproach me; while they continually say unto me, "Where is thy God?" '

Yet it is a question we must answer. We cannot avoid it like the boy of twelve who said: 'Some boys in my class are for marriage; some are against it; I'm neutral.' No man can be neutral here. Pascal wrote: 'It is certain either that God is or that He is not: there is no medium point . . . you must wager: this is not a matter of choice; you are committed, and not to wager that God is is to wager that He is not. Which side then do you take?' Jesus said: 'He that is not for me is against me.'

When spring-cleaning a room, a woman begins by clearing out the furniture. We too must clear the ground and ask: 'What sort of a proof of God do men expect?' If they expect a knock-down proof in five minutes, like the proof that 2 and 2 make 4, it can't be done. No really big question can be settled like that. No man can prove that his wife loves him that way. What we can do is to show that Christianity fits all the facts better than anything else.

The first fact is that we cannot know all the facts.

Isaac Newton reminded his contemporaries that his vast knowledge was only like a few pebbles picked up on the shore of the sea of truth; and any man who rejects God because there are gaps here and there in our understanding is a shallow thinker. A modern mathematician with theories about the universe was asked, 'If you have described a thing have you explained it?' 'Certainly,' he replied. He might have learned from Newton; the wise man is the man who perceives the mystery about him with a sense of awe, who sits down before the order, beauty and purpose of the universe and asks: 'Why is this here?' The teenage girl awe-struck by the sight of a great oak is on the edge of discoveries about God. She is like a man who, coming out of a planetarium, said: 'There's more than chance behind that; there's mind in it.'

The second fact is that though doubt may lodge in our intellect, faith demands the whole personality—will, choice, decision, affection, as well as intellect.

A man may effectively cling to God without being able to put every piece of the jig-saw in its place. George MacDonald said: 'A man may be haunted with doubt and thereby grow to faith.' To try God is the only way: 'O taste and see that the Lord is good' (Psalm 34[8]).

The third fact is that we cannot conceive, explain or picture God except in human terms.

This is both a difficulty and deliverance; for God is not as we are, and yet this is a way of understanding Him. Being human, we explain everything in terms of ourselves: 'I looked into the eye of the sun', we say. The danger is that, making God in our image, we may think Him insignificant like us. To express God in terms of man is like trying to explain to a mouse, in terms of mice, what it is to be a man. This difficulty, which is from man's side insurmountable, is also our deliverance, for it is at this point that God has taken the initiative and revealed Himself in His Son, Jesus. This is the record of the New Testament.

A group of students were once discussing the life and writings of Kagawa of Japan. They had all read of him, but one was able to say: 'I've had a meal with him.' The first disciples of Jesus could say the same, and could add from experience: 'In Him dwelleth all the fulness of the Godhead bodily' (Col 2[9]). What men had glimpsed of God they saw fulfilled in Christ. God's demanding holiness, His love and care for 'every child of man', all beauty, truth and love, come to full flower in Christ, and they said: 'No man hath seen God at any time; the only begotten Son, . . . He hath declared Him' (John 1[18]). When we look at Calvary we see, not a proposition, but a face, and the face is the face of God.

It is for this reason that to look at Calvary has helped men to believe in God and bear their own calvaries. An American sergeant, flogged and starved by the Japanese, said: 'They were ignorant and mean . . . so I am going to a missionary school and then I'm going to Japan for the rest of my life to teach them the importance of Love among men.' The same view of Calvary inspired the Christians of Cyprian's Africa in the third century to help their persecutors in the time of plague; for, said Cyprian, 'We must be worthy of our birth'. They had looked at Calvary and seen that 'God, who . . . spake in time past unto the fathers by the prophets, hath in these last days spoken unto us by his Son' (Hebrews 1^{1}).

BOOK LIST: *Books on this subject are legion. Here are some cheap ones:*

Mere Christianity, C. S. Lewis (Fontana, 2*s.* 6*d.*).
Christian Doctrine, J. S. Whale (Fontana, 2*s.* 6*d.*).
The Christian's God, Wm. Neill (World Christian Books, 2*s.*).

A FORTNIGHT'S DEVOTIONAL READING FROM THE BIBLE AND 'METHODIST HYMN-BOOK' ON THIS SUBJECT

Day	*Bible*	*MHB*
1	Mark 1^{14-15}; Romans 10^{6-9}	530
2	Matthew 8^{5-13}	502
3	John 1^{10-13}; 1 Timothy 6^{6-12}	70
4	John 6^{64-71}, 16^{29-33}	510
5	John 14^{8-14}	518
6	Habakkuk 2^{4}; John 20^{26-32}	527
7	Acts 15^{6-11}	368
8	Psalm 46; Romans 1^{8-17}	494
9	Psalm 121; Romans 3^{19-30}	497
10	Romans 5^{1-11}	354
11	Ephesians 2^{1-9}; Hebrews 6^{1-12}	375
12	Isaiah 43^{1-7}; Galatians 5^{1-6}	500
13	Hebrews 11^{1-16}	532
14	Hebrews 11^{17}–12^{2}	507

QUESTIONS FOR DISCUSSION

(1) Do evolution and history lead us to God or away from Him?
(2) 'Our Lord came among us not to clear up perplexity but to show us which side to take.'
What do we mean by faith—certainty or trust?
(3) 'Many are called but few are chosen.' Why do men doubt?

PRAYER

O ALMIGHTY God, who alone canst order the unruly wills and affections of sinful men: Grant unto Thy people, that they may love the thing which Thou commandest, and desire that which Thou dost promise; that so, among the sundry and manifold changes of the world, our hearts may surely there be fixed, where true joys are to be found; through Jesus Christ our Lord. *Amen.*

TWO

Jesus: Son of God

THE FIRST question the disciples asked about Jesus was: 'Who then is this, that even the wind and the sea obey him?' (Mark 4[41]) —and the whole New Testament gives the astonishing answer: 'God was in Christ reconciling the world to Himself.' At first, however, the disciples were only sure of one thing, namely that *Jesus was a man.* They knew this, not from the Creed as we do, but from experience. They saw Him eat and drink; they saw Him hungry. They knew where He came from, for He was 'of the seed of Abraham'. They saw His joy, His anger, His endurance, His courage. They heard the note of admiration in the voice of Pilate: 'Behold the man'—and 'What a man', Pilate seemed to say. They heard from Jesus of the temptations in the desert, and knew they could only have been real temptations if He had been capable of falling before them like other men. They had no doubt that He was a real, flesh-and-blood man. Turgenev once wrote: 'I saw myself a boy in a low-pitched wooden church. All at once a man came up from behind and stood beside me. I did not turn towards Him, but I felt that the man was Christ. Emotion, curiosity, awe overmastered me. I made an effort and looked at my neighbour. A face like everyone's; a face like all men's faces. "What sort of Christ is this"? I thought; "such an ordinary, ordinary man. It cannot be." I turned away; but I had hardly turned my eyes from this ordinary man when I felt again that it was none other than Christ standing beside me. Only then I realized that just such a face is the face of Christ—a face like all men's faces.' There are few today who would deny this unless, against all the evidence, they deny that Jesus lived; but there are many who can accept the appeal of Christ to their conscience without being convinced of the second truth which overwhelmed the disciples, that *Jesus was God.* Men sometimes ask: 'Was Christ simply a peg on which His followers, especially Paul, hung their ideas?' The more we study the record the more unsatisfactory this view seems. Consider that—

(*a*) The first believers were Jews. Peter, who said, 'Thou art the Christ, the Son of the Living God', was a Jew. Thomas, who said, 'My Lord and my God', was a Jew. Paul, who wrote, 'God sent his own Son in the likeness of sinful flesh', and He 'is the image of the invisible God', was a Jew. John, who wrote, 'And the Word became flesh and dwelt among us (and we beheld his glory, the glory as of the only begotten from the Father)', was a Jew. The significance of this fact is only fully realized when we remember that a Jew would rather die than accept that any man or image could take the place of God. 'Thou shalt have no other Gods before me . . .' said the Law; 'Thou shalt not make unto thee any graven image or any likeness . . .'. The Jews were fanatics about this, and Paul was one of the most fanatical. Yet he was convinced that in the man Jesus he saw God. He was what God meant by 'man'; He was what man meant by 'God'. What is more—

(*b*) This claim went back to JESUS Himself. There is no doubt that Jesus saw Himself as fulfilling in His person a unique mission from God. He came 'preaching the Kingdom (or Rule) of God'. In Him the power of God was concentrated: 'If I by the finger of God cast out devils, then is the Kingdom of God come upon you' (Luke 11[20]). Both at His Baptism and Transfiguration there was direct testimony: 'This is my beloved Son, hear him', and it was but a short step to the full-orbed claim which the disciples accepted at the Last Supper, the Cross and the empty tomb: 'I and the Father are one. . . . He that hath seen me hath seen the Father.'

If we ask how these things can be, we are only expressing the wonder of every human soul before the mystery of God in Christ. Forsyth explains it in this way: 'God and man meet in humanity . . . as two movements in mutual interplay . . . on the one hand we have an initiative, creative, productive action, clear and sure on the part of the eternal and absolute God; on the other hand we have the seeking, receptive, appropriating action of groping, erring, growing man . . . all spiritual history is action . . . if the whole drama of the soul of man could be compressed into one narrow neck and one strait gate, that is what we should have—the most tremendous friction of these two currents within a personal experience.' The 'drama' *is* so compressed in Christ; the 'friction' culminates in the Cross. But this is not where *we* begin; we begin at the lake-side: 'He comes to us as One unknown, without a name, as of old by the lake-side', writes Schweitzer. 'He speaks to us the same words "Follow Me" and sets us to the tasks which He has to fulfil for our time. To those who obey Him . . . He will reveal Himself in the toils, conflicts and sufferings which they shall pass through in His fellowship, and as an ineffable mystery, they shall learn in their own experience who He is.'

BOOK LIST

The best books on this subject are the GOSPELS: but if you want help in reading them try William Barclay's *Daily Study Bible*. Each Gospel costs about 5*s*.
You might also try *Who Is Jesus Christ*, Wm. Neill (World Christian Books, 2*s*. 6*d*.).

A FORTNIGHT'S DEVOTIONAL READING FROM THE BIBLE AND 'METHODIST HYMN-BOOK' ON THIS SUBJECT

Day	*Bible*	*MHB*
1	Genesis 1; John 1^{1-8}	86
2	Deuteronomy 4^{14-24}; Ephesians 1^{10-23}	126
3	Nehemiah 8^{13-18}; Mark 9^{2-8}	140
4	Psalm 2; Mark 1^{1-15}	339
5	Psalm 8; 1 Corinthians 15^{20-8}	88
6	Psalm 16; Ephesians 1^{15-23}	445
7	Psalm 89; Colossians 1^{9-23}	135
8	Psalm 107; Mark 4^{35-41}	223
9	Psalm 110; Hebrews 1	830
10	Isaiah 8^{14}; 1 Peter 2^{1-10}	65
11	Isaiah 42^{1-9}; Philip 2^{5-11}	117
12	Daniel 7^{13-14}; Mark 8^{27}–9^{1}	96
13	Zachariah 9^{17}; Luke 19^{24-40}	134
14	Zachariah 13^{7-9}; John 10^{1-18}	174

QUESTIONS FOR DISCUSSION

(1) The humanist says: 'Jesus was only a man, though a good man.' Could such a faith have won the world?

(2) 'Christianity is the most materialistic of all religions', said William Temple. But the world thinks it a myth, a mirage. Beginning with Christmas, illustrate what Temple said.

PRAYERS OF INTERCESSION AND ADORATION

'Lord, I believe; help Thou mine unbelief.'
'Lord have mercy on me, a sinner.'
('What would'st thou?') 'Lord, that I might receive my sight.'
'Truly this man was a Son of God.'
'My Lord and my God.'
'Who art Thou, Lord?' ('I am Jesus whom thou persecutest').

THREE

Jesus the Saviour

'MEN OF the world' sometimes say that if only Christians would look at life, the ivory tower of their faith would, like a rotten tooth, crumble before 'reality'. Is this so? Who is the more realistic, the Christian or the 'man of the world'? Consider what each has to say about MAN. The 'man of the world' is optimistic; if there is anything wrong with man (says he) it can be traced to his present ignorance, his environment, or his genes and chromosomes. Man's moral progress is a matter of time. This, replies the Christian, is naïve, 'as if you were to point out to an old lady at a garden party that there was an escaped lion twenty yards away . . . and she said, "Oh yes," and took another cucumber sandwich'.

The Christian is also optimistic about men, but for a different reason. His optimism is in God, for man is God's creature, made in His image. Only so can man's flashes of glory be explained. As Chesterton pointed out, we encourage a fallen man by saying, 'Be a man'; we point him to his discarded greatness. We don't discourage a crocodile from eating a missionary by saying 'Be a crocodile'. Man is made in God's image, says the Christian; but he adds with realism—man has repudiated that image; he is a sinner. His liberty has become bondage, the image of man's 'godalmightyness'. The prodigal has not become a pig, but he has become a slave. Genesis 1 and 2 describe how man tries to displace God as the centre of the picture. 'We are all born doing this', said William Temple. This is what the Church means by 'original' sin; it is in our origin.

This 'Fall' is often denied. Darwin's *Origin of Species* (1859) described it as a 'climb'. Herbert Spencer wrote: 'Progress is not an accident but a necessity . . . it is part of nature.' The hollowness of such naïve optimism was revealed in the first World War. After it men sought to escape from the world they had made—to Australia; in dancing the Charleston; in pursuit of the 'bright young thing'. But men's troubles went with them. Education or science next became man's hope; but Belsen and the other concentration camps showed that man could be educated for evil, and science produced the atom bomb. In the 1930's many had despaired—

We are the hollow men,
We are the stuffed men.
Standing together
Headpieces stuffed with straw.

So T. S. Eliot had written; and he had prophesied: 'This is the way the world ends, not with a bang but a whimper.' It seemed he might be right. One by one the nations fell victim, between the wars, to the barbarism they had created. In 1945 hope fluttered its brief wings:

There'll be bluebirds over
The white cliffs of Dover
Tomorrow, just you wait and see.

Friendship with Russia was established by a pact of fifty years. Enthusiasm was high. It has all evaporated in Hungary, the shadow of the Sputnik, and the cloud of the Hydrogen bomb. Whether or not the 'man in the street' is ready to recognize MAN for what he is—Dr Jekyll *and* Mr Hyde—the Christian must be realistic. We have no hope in ourselves; 'Our sufficiency is of God.'

When a man repents he finds hope in the Cross of Christ: 'A contrite heart, O God, Thou wilt not despise.'

Two things must be added:

(1) *Only God* CAN *save; and God* WILL *save*

God begins by forgiving us at the Cross. 'A righteousness of God is revealed . . .', says Paul. He didn't mean a 'goody-goody-ness' but a power that puts us right. Christ accepts us as we are. Paul, Luther, Wesley all tried to save themselves and failed. It was when they knelt at the Cross that they found peace. Luther said: 'The forgiveness of sins ought to make you rejoice; it is the very heart of Christianity.' God can save; God will save; God has saved. Sin and death, which defeat us, Christ has defeated. The concentrated powers of darkness conspired to overcome God's love, and God won. 'It is accomplished', Jesus said, and the disciples were witnesses of the Resurrection and cried: 'The sting of death is sin . . . but thanks be to God, who giveth us the victory.'

(2) *Man must respond*

The Jew responded in sacrifice, and he identified himself with his offering. After 2,000 years of Christianity this is strange to us, but the idea filled the mind of Christ as He went to the Cross.

'Behold the Lamb of God that taketh away the sin of the world', John the Baptist had said, and Jesus thought of Isaiah 53: 'He was despised and rejected . . . as a sheep before her shearers is dumb so he opened not his mouth . . . by his stripes we are healed.' In Christ, humanity, perfect as it has never been, made a perfect offering of obedience to God.

'He bore the sin of many.' How else can we understand the Cry of Dereliction—'My God, my God, why hast thou forsaken me?'—except to say that Christ bore the burden of our sin as if it were His own, and felt Himself cut off from God as we are? We can never plumb the depths of that cry; He took the cup of this world's sin and drained it to the dregs. When we by faith 'accept' Him, we share in His obedience, and we become 'sons of God'.

BOOK LIST

The world is full of books on this subject, but you might borrow W. R. Maltby's *The Meaning of the Cross* (Epworth Press). So much is there put in so little space.

A FORTNIGHT'S DEVOTIONAL READING FROM THE BIBLE AND 'METHODIST HYMN-BOOK' ON THIS SUBJECT

Day	*Bible*	*MHB*
1	1 Thessalonians 5^{1-11}	75
2	Titus 3^{1-7}	99
3	2 Timothy 1^{16-14}	97
4	John 3^{14-21}	110
5	Acts 4^{5-12}	114
6	Hebrews 2^{1-11}	115
7	Romans 1^{14-17}, 3^{21-8}	262
8	2 Corinthians 5^{20}–6^{12}	Verse 17
9	Ephesians 2^{1-10}	200
10	Philippians 2^{12-18}	202
11	1 Corinthians 1^{17-25}	203
12	Mark 15^{21-39}	191
13	Luke 23^{32-43}	184
14	John 19^{16-30}	181

QUESTIONS FOR DISCUSSION

(1) The Church says you are a sinner; the psychologist says you are maladjusted. Who is right? Is there any difference?
(2) 'The Cross will be in the heart of God until the end of time.' What does this mean? Could the world have been saved without it?
(3) 'Work out your own salvation with fear and trembling' (Phil 2[12]). 'Nothing in my hands I bring, Simply to Thy Cross I cling.' Reconcile these if possible.

PRAYER

Jesus, the First and Last,
On Thee my soul is cast:
Thou didst Thy work begin
By blotting out my sin;
Thou wilt the root remove,
And perfect me in love.

FOUR

The Resurrection

ON 10TH JANUARY, 1958 the Young Communist League commented from Moscow on the Dead Sea Scrolls—the first mention since they were discovered in 1947. 'They give', they said, 'conclusive proof of the mythical character of Jesus . . . they explain the contradictions and absurdities in Holy Writ.' There was no mention of the Resurrection in the passage quoted, but no doubt this would be dismissed as even more absurd. *Yet* the Resurrection is the starting-point of the Christian Church and our faith. When Bishop Azariah of Dornakal was asked where one should begin with a young convert, he answered: 'With the Resurrection.' It was good advice, because it was at this point of experience that the first preachers began. 'Whom God raised up, having loosed the pangs of death . . . !', said Peter on the day of Pentecost (Acts 2[24]). It was here they ended. Paul said to Festus: 'Touching the resurrection of the dead, I am called in question' (Acts 24[21], 26[23]). The Resurrection is the beginning and the end of our faith. What then is the evidence about it for twentieth-century man?

Before 1939 a young lad from land-locked Bavaria stayed with a family by the sea-side. He had never seen the sea but he was taken swimming. He swallowed a mouthful. 'It's salty', he shouted incredulously. He had been warned but he hadn't believed it. It was such direct, personal experience which changed Saul the persecutor into Paul the Apostle. 'Have not I also seen the Lord?' he asked. Only a tremendous thing like the Resurrection could account for the change in Paul and the other disciples. 'Rabbits were changed into ferrets.' What could have done it? Only the Resurrection.

Consider the disciples on the night after Calvary—fear in every face, dejection, nothing to live for. Consider the same men again a few weeks later after they had received the gift of the Spirit—out in the streets aflame with confidence, words ringing like iron, absolutely fearless and happy, planning the conquest of the world. What did it? By whom did the Spirit come? 'He was crucified, dead and buried . . . ; the third day He rose again from the dead.' That was it. Perhaps you have seen those strong-man advertisements featured in boys' magazines: 'You too can have a body like mine.' With the blurb are a couple of contrasting pictures: BEFORE, an eight-stone weakling; AFTER, a miracle-man with bulging muscles. Before . . . after. So it was with the Church, and only the Resurrection could have done it. This is our faith.

Not everyone accepts this, however, so let us list some of the objections which have been raised (and refuted) from the earliest days. The critics have said:

(1) '*The story was invented.*' 'There are differences in the Gospel accounts.' 'His disciples . . . stole Him away' (Matthew 28[13]). Three things may be said in reply:

(*a*) The differences make us more certain the accounts are true. Five word-for-word accounts of a football match from five different people would sound very much like collaboration and invention. When Hannibal crossed the Alps the historians Livy and Polybius could not agree on which pass he used. Does it matter? We know he was at one time North of the Alps and at another South. The fact is sure. So with the Resurrection, the differences show the human reporter's viewpoint; the fact is sure.

(*b*) If the Church had invented the Resurrection, could it have lived and grown with such a lie at its heart? What did the disciples gain by 'inventing' it? Only the block, the faggot and the lion.

(*c*) Stealing His body was impossible (see below the comment on the 'Empty Tomb').

(2) '*He only swooned on the Cross and recovered in the grave*'

Those who knew what crucifixion was like didn't invent this one. What of the spear thrust? Could such a mangled man, if He did only faint, have rolled the stone away, broken the seal, overcome the guard . . . ? It's unthinkable. Could such a man have convinced the Church that He was the 'Lord of Life'? Unthinkable again.

(3) '*His disciples saw a vision*'

But visions don't arise unless the 'seers' are psychologically prepared; and nothing could be less true of the disciples. They went to Jerusalem expecting a triumph, and they found the Cross. This shattered them. They expected nothing more, but went back to their fishing. Far from expecting anything, they were the first who had to be convinced of the Resurrection. 'Doubting Thomas' was in no mood for seeing things. They did not accept the Resurrection easily, but 'then were the disciples glad *when they saw the Lord*' (John 20^{20}).

There is another *fact* we must consider: the *Empty Tomb*.

Because of the approaching Passover, Jesus was crucified in a hurry and buried in a hurry (without the usual embalming) because it was unlawful to carry anything on the 'Sabbath', i.e. Saturday. They buried Him at 6 p.m. on Friday, and by first light, or in other words at the first moment they could, the women carried spices to the tomb, wondering who would roll the stone away for them. When they got there, they found the stone rolled away, the guard gone and the tomb empty save for the grave-clothes—a silent and complete witness to the Resurrection.

If Saul the persecutor, or Annas or Caiaphas had wanted to kill the infant Church stone dead, they had only to produce the corpse. They couldn't do it. There wasn't a corpse—only some grave-clothes. No wonder Peter said on the day of Pentecost, 'This Jesus did God raise up, whereof we are witnesses' (Acts 2^{32}).

No wonder thousands believed and joined the Church, and still do.

BOOK LIST

Who Moved the Stone, by Morrison, can now be obtained in a paper-back for a few shillings. It is a story of detection and reads like a book by Agatha Christie. Morrison set out to prove that the Resurrection never happened and was forced by the facts to prove that it had.

A FORTNIGHT'S DEVOTIONAL READING FROM THE BIBLE AND 'METHODIST HYMN-BOOK' ON THIS SUBJECT

Day	*Bible*	*MHB*
1	1 Corinthians 15$^{1-19}$	205
2	Romans 8$^{31-9}$	207
3	Mark 10^{34}, 16$^{1-8}$	210
4	Matthew 27$^{62-6}$	212
5	Luke 24$^{13-35}$	217

6	John 20	218
7	John 21	219
8	Acts 1^{1-11}	222
9	Acts 4^{5-22}	225
10	Acts 26^{1-29}	227
11	Philippians 3^{8-14}	229
12	1 Peter $1^{3-9, 21}$	231
13	Hebrews 13^{20-1}	661
14	Revelation 1^{1-8}	195

QUESTIONS FOR DISCUSSION

(1) The New Testament preachers always begin with the Resurrection. Is this true? (See Acts.)

(2) Assume for the moment that Jesus didn't rise from the dead. Would the New Testament or the Church have been possible?

(3) 'Dead men tell no tales' says our modern age. Yet it is an age of 'miracles'. Consider the miracle of birth; is there anything impossible in the miracle of resurrection?

A FIRST-CENTURY PRAYER OF THANKSGIVING FROM THE DIDACHE

We give Thee thanks, Holy Father, for Thy holy Name, which Thou hast made to tabernacle in our hearts, for the knowledge and faith and immortality, which Thou hast made known to us through Thy Son Jesus. . . . Thou didst give us food and drink for enjoyment, that we might render thanks to Thee; but didst bestow upon us spiritual food and drink and eternal life through Thy Son. Maran Atha. *Amen.*

FIVE

The Word of God

IT IS BECAUSE the Bible is a word about God's redemption, a word about Jesus, that it has its unique place in Christian faith and worship. John Wesley was glad to be called 'a man of one book', and Methodist ministers today are asked at ordination: 'Are you persuaded that the Holy Scriptures contain sufficiently all doctrine necessary for eternal salvation . . . ? And are you determined, out of the said Scriptures to instruct the people committed to your charge; and to teach nothing, as required of necessity for eternal salvation, but that which you shall be persuaded may be concluded and proved by the Scriptures?' This is why we should treasure the Bible. But there are other reasons:

(*a*) *Convincing preaching has no other basis*

As the disciples walked to Emmaus (Luke 24) Jesus 'interpreted to them in all the scriptures the things concerning himself', and afterwards they said: 'Was not our heart burning within us, . . . while he opened to us the scriptures?' Wesley's heart, too, was strangely warmed when 'one read Luther's *Preface to the Romans*'. The Bible has always been the gateway to conversion, and today still, 'the seed is the word'.

(*b*) *Many died that we might have it*

'I will make a boy who drives a plough to know more of the Scriptures than the King of England', said Tyndale. He succeeded, but he died at the stake. It cost thirteen shillings and tenpence to burn Latimer and Ridley. So cheap to burn, so dearly bought.

(*c*) *Our civilization is based on it*

'It lives on the ear like music that can never be forgotten, . . . it is part of the national mind and the anchor of national seriousness.'

Therefore men have studied it, prayed with it, written commentaries on it, and made it their rule of faith and conduct. At Worms, Luther refused to recant, 'Unless I am proved wrong by the testimony of scripture'. By this testimony we today also test our faith.

Before we go on to ask wherein lies the authority of scripture we must face a modern problem. Many sincere Christians claim for the book itself an absolute and unconditional authority. They claim, for example, that the Bible is *verbally* inspired and that any modern scientific theory must be wrong which is at variance with it. The world, for example, must have been made in six days of twenty-four hours, whatever science says. Sometimes they add: 'If one part of the Bible can be proved wrong, the whole must fall to the ground.' They have been called 'Fundamentalists', and they have called those who take the other view—that the work of scientific research on the text and transmission of scripture is valuable—'Modernists'. For them a word of 1861 would express the truth: 'The Bible is none other than the Word of God, not some part of it more, some part of it less, but all alike the utterance of Him that sitteth upon the throne, faultless, unerring, supreme.'

While recognizing their sincerity, their love of Jesus, the high position they give the Bible and their desire for certainty, most Christians today reject this view. They do so for the following reasons:

(*a*) There are irreconcilable contradictions within the Bible itself in matters of detail—two differing accounts of the creation, two dates of the Last Supper, two accounts of the healing of blind Bartimaeus—one saying he was healed before and one after Jesus came to Jericho (Mark 10^{46}, Luke 18^{35}, 19^{1}).

(*b*) The fundamentalist view puts all scriptures on the same level. Jesus Himself did not do this; in the Sermon on the Mount His words supersede the Old Testament. St Paul also gives more authority to 'a word from the Lord' than he does to his own writings.

(*c*) It denies that growth in the understanding of God to which the Bible bears witness.

(*d*) It opens the door to an obsolete morality. Slavery has been defended from Genesis 9.

(*e*) Most tragically, it is the greatest stumbling-block to faith for thousands, who, brought up in this scientific age, must (if they take this view) keep their Christian faith in one compartment and the rest of life in another. Dr Marcus Dods said of it fifty years ago: 'No doctrine more surely manufactures sceptics.'

This view is of recent growth, for scholarship in the Church from the earliest days has agreed that the Bible is not a book about science, or geology, or ancient history, but a book about God. It is the record of how God revealed Himself to men, and how men understood Him, at first 'through a glass darkly' and then 'face-to-face'. It is an interpretation and an invitation.

Does this take away its authority? By no means. Its authority is in the Spirit and not in the letter. 'Every scripture *inspired* of God is also profitable' says 2 Timothy 3^{16}. The word is 'inspired' not '*dictated*'. God did not neutralize the intellect of those He inspired; their inspiration is as various as their Greek. The Holy Spirit is no more responsible for their mistakes in detail than He is for their bad grammar. What is important is that those who wrote the Bible received the message of the love of God and transmitted it. The transmitter and receiver may both be weak, but the message gets over.

The Holy Spirit who gave it to them reinterprets it in our hearts. Herein is its authority. 'The Holy Scripture is not a book which can be interpreted apart from the Holy Spirit by whom it came.'

Let St Augustine speak for all scholars: 'God Himself, because He is the Light, enlighteneth religious minds that they may understand divine truths that are declared. . . . God hath created man's mind rational and intellectual, whereby man may take in His light . . . and He so enlighteneth it of Himself that not only those things which are displayed by the truth but even the truth itself may be perceived by the mind's eye.'

BOOK LIST

A Plain Man Looks at the Bible, Wm. Neill (Fontana, 2*s*.).
Fundamentalism and the Bible, F. Glasson (Epworth, 9*d*.).
Biblical Preaching and Biblical Scholarship, C. K. Barrett (Epworth, 9*d*.).

A FORTNIGHT'S DEVOTIONAL READING FROM THE BIBLE AND 'METHODIST HYMN-BOOK' ON THIS SUBJECT

Day	*Bible*	*MHB*
1	Psalm 119^{105-12}	78
2	Isaiah 55^{6-13}	302
3	Jeremiah 36^{20-9}	303
4	Luke 24^{13-35}	304

5	Luke 24$^{44-9}$	68
6	John 1$^{1-14}$	306
7	John 5$^{30-47}$	307
8	John 14$^{23-31}$	308
9	John 16$^{7-15}$	309
10	Acts 8$^{26-40}$	310
11	Acts 13$^{44-52}$	782
12	2 Timothy 3$^{10-17}$	548
13	1 Peter 1$^{13-25}$	562
14	Revelation 22$^{10-19}$	677

QUESTIONS FOR DISCUSSION

(1) Do you agree or disagree with the argument of this chapter?

(2) It has been asked: 'Why don't we get rid of the Old Testament?' Why don't we?

(3) Did the Bible produce the Church, or the Church the Bible? Is either infallible? Where does authority lie for the Christian?

PRAYER

Blessed Lord, who hast caused all Holy Scriptures to be written for our learning: Grant that we may in such wise hear them, read, mark, learn and inwardly digest them, that by patience, and comfort of Thy holy Word, we may embrace, and ever hold fast the blessed hope of everlasting life, which Thou hast given us in our Saviour Jesus Christ. *Amen.*

SIX

The Holy Spirit

THE HOLY SPIRIT is given a small place in the *Te Deum* and an equally small place in the minds of most Christians. This may be because the thinking of the Church on this subject was interrupted when the Roman world fell into decline and men have only taken up the strain sporadically since. It may also be for two other reasons:

(*a*) The terms in which we think of the Spirit are confusing. Fatherhood is familiar in our experience; Sonship is something we all know a little about; but 'Spirit' and 'Ghost' conjure up ideas far removed from God—'The headless spectre of the moated grange'. Nor is Dove much better. We sympathize with the oriental who said: 'Heavenly Father, O.K.; Heavenly Son, O.K.; but Holy Pigeon—I don't get it.'

(*b*) Certain experiences can only be understood when we have had them ourselves. If you have fallen in love, love takes on a meaning which you only dimly understood before. Parenthood, if you become a parent, will make you fond of a jammy-faced baby . . . to the astonishment sometimes of the childless. Similarly, the doctrine of the Holy Spirit is only dull if you don't know Him. Sermons about Him are like sermons about breathing. If you can breathe there is no need for you to be told how to do it; if you can't breathe you won't hear the sermon.

The men at Ephesus (Acts 19) were honest, repentant and devout, but there was no thrill in their religion. They didn't know the Holy Spirit. They would not have been able to appreciate the letter F. D. Maurice wrote to his fiancée a hundred years ago: 'I should like to be with you on Whit Sunday, but this year we must be content to wish each other the infinite blessings of it at a distance.' Would most Christians today appreciate such a letter?

By His Spirit, God created the world, and inspired His prophets, like fierce winds from the desert, to speak to the political situation of their day. By His Spirit, God promised to breathe life into the dry bones of Israel (Ezekiel 37). That promise was fulfilled in the work of the Holy Spirit in the conception of Jesus (Luke 1[35]), in His baptism as God's 'beloved son' (Mark 1[11]), and in His Cross and Resurrection. At Pentecost the prayer of Moses, 'would God that all the Lord's people were prophets, and that the Lord would put his spirit upon them!', was answered for the whole Church. Whenever the Spirit of God has come upon the Church certain signs have followed. These are—

(1) *Conversion.* The Spirit of God is responsible for that 'change of mind' we call conversion. We trace His work in Chapters 8-11 of Acts. A certain pattern is seen in each account. Paul, Cornelius, the Ethiopian, all strove for faith; each man prayed and searched the scriptures—and each man waited. As he waited the Spirit acted within him. Today, where men are converted, the same applies. In 1936 the Uganda Synod of the Church of England wrote: 'All members of the Church . . . must know in their lives the meaning of being "born again". It is not possible to change others until we ourselves are changed. Ask yourselves: "Do I know salvation through the Cross: am I growing in the Holy Spirit, in prayer, in knowledge of God . . . ?"' The revival which followed stood the test of Mau Mau in 1953.

(2) *Holiness.* Jesus said 'By their fruits you shall know them', and one of the clearest proofs of the truth and effectiveness of our faith is that it produces saints. These are men and women in whom the Spirit of God has been at work so long and so completely that they "are changed . . . from glory to glory'.

(3) *Witness.* The first expression of Pentecost was open-air preaching. Jesus had promised: 'You shall be my witnesses . . . when the Holy Ghost is come upon you.' It is still true today. A circuit commission stood on a hill overlooking a new estate; the Spirit touched them with vision. 'We must go in there', they said. And they did.

(4) *Unity.* The early Church broke down barriers which had existed for centuries. They 'had all things common', women were equal with men, there was 'neither Jew nor Greek', bond nor free, colour bar did not exist and master and slave were one at the Lord's table. How often has this been forgotten, not only a hundred years ago—when chapels were built with cushions and carpets for the masters, thinner cushions and lino for the foremen, and bare boards for the workers—but today when we cannot come together at the place where we all lose our pride and our distinction, the Lord's table! When Jesus asked for the gift of the Spirit for His disciples (John 17) He asked 'that they might all be one . . . that the world might know that thou did'st send me'.

The Holy Spirit, therefore, is God at work in the Church

today. What does He wish of the Church? That it should fulfil the proud names given to it in the New Testament. These are (to mention only the most important of them):

(1) *The People of God.* Like the Jews, the Church was chosen by God to bear a distinctive witness. We are still the people of 'the Way'. The Church is 'a colony of Heaven', and like an embassy in an alien land the customs and character of the mother country are found in it.

(2) *The Fellowship.* The Church is not an exclusive group of like-minded people who happen to like each other. It is an open society on earth and in heaven with no limits. Its task is 'to seek and to save that which was lost'.

(3) *The Body of Christ.* As Christ took flesh 2,000 years ago, so His Spirit is incarnate in us today. 'We are His hands through which He does His work today.' So the Church loves and serves the community in which it finds itself. Just as the incarnation of Jesus involved Him in the Cross, so the Church must suffer today to do His will, for the world still says with Nietzsche: 'I will not believe in the Redeemer of the Christians until they show me they are redeemed.'

BOOK LIST

C. H. Dodd, *The Meaning of Paul for Today* (Fontana, 2*s.* 6*d.*), Chap. 10.

A FORTNIGHT'S DEVOTIONAL READING FROM THE BIBLE AND 'METHODIST HYMN-BOOK' ON THIS SUBJECT

Day	*Bible*	*MHB*
1	Judges 3$^{7-11}$	305
2	Numbers 11$^{23-9}$	377
3	Micah 3	554
4	Isaiah 61	730
5	Luke 1$^{15, 35, 41, 67}$	765
6	Luke 3$^{16-22}$	273
7	Luke 4$^{1-14}$	274
8	Acts 2$^{1-21}$	275
9	Acts 10$^{34-48}$	278
10	Romans 5$^{1-8}$	280
11	2 Corinthians 5$^{1-10}$	284
12	Galatians 5^{16}–6^{1}	292
13	1 Corinthians 12–14	299
14	John 16$^{1-15}$	301

QUESTIONS FOR DISCUSSION

(1) What is conversion? Is it necessary to be converted to be a Christian?

(2) The Spirit of God is driving the Church towards unity. Would you be willing to give up anything for unity? If so what? (Do you feel like criticizing the wording of this question?)

(3) Every heretic has claimed that he has direct guidance from the Spirit. What are the dangers of this doctrine? How can we guard against them?

PRAYER

Come Holy Ghost, our hearts inspire. As we invoke Thee, make us ready for the glorious pain of being caught by Thy power out of our petty orbit into the eternal purposes of the Almighty, in whose onward sweep our lives are as a speck of dust. *Amen.*

SEVEN

The Commandments

of Moses
of the Lord Jesus
Wesley's Rules

IN HIS BOOK, *Concerning Christian Liberty*, Luther wrote: 'The Christian man is absolute free lord of all, subject to none . . . his royal power rules over all things.' But when he was challenged at the peril of his life to state the limits of his own freedom, he replied: 'My conscience is bound by the Word of God; it is neither safe nor honest to act against one's conscience.' Many men claim freedom today without accepting these limits laid down by Luther—that a man should be bound by a conscience ruled over by the Word of God. But freedom without this is licence.

For the Christian man, however, there is much in God's word to direct his conscience: in the Old Testament we find the Ten Commandments (Exodus 20^{1-17}), and even the Code of Deuteronomy (12–26) and the Law of Holiness (Leviticus 17–26) may be of some help. In the New Testament there are the Sermon on the Mount (Matthew 5–7) and the later chapters of the Epistles.

But there is danger in all 'codes', for in the hands of men they may become fossilized. This happened to the Jewish Law: the Jewish tailor was forbidden to put his needle into his lapel any evening of the week lest on the eve of the sabbath he forgot it and 'bore a burden' into his house, so profaning the day. His life was ruled by 613 negatives, and thirty-nine types of work were forbidden on the Sabbath. The Law was meant to protect things spiritual, but it became 'death'. A choking hedge was built round everything, and who can say that such a hedge has not occasionally been built round the Christian? 'Methodists,' someone asked, 'aren't they the people who are always saying, "Don't do this, and don't do that?"' With this danger goes another danger: that such legalism may breed two heresies:

(*a*) That we believe we can save ourselves. 'I've kept the rules today; I shall be all right'; or, put in another way: 'Why should this happen to him; he never did anyone any harm?'

(*b*) That we bargain with God. (Consider Genesis 28^{20-2}.)

It is only when we turn to Jesus that we find deliverance from this. 'I am not come to destroy [the law and the prophets], but to fulfil', He said, and He replaced the dead letter with the living principle of love. When faced with a crippled woman (Luke 13) the Jew could allow healing on the Sabbath only if it saved life or relieved extreme pain. Hers was not an extreme case. 'There are six days in which work ought to be done', said the ruler of the synagogue; 'therefore in them come and be healed, and not on the sabbath day'. He stuck close to the letter of the law; but Jesus, in replying to him, stuck close to the principle of love: 'You on the sabbath loose your ox and ass from the stall, ought not this woman . . . whom Satan hath bound . . . to be loosed from this bond on the day of the sabbath?'

In the Holy Communion Service we repeat the Commandments of the Lord Jesus. They are all about love:

Love God . . .
Love thy neighbour . . .
Love one another . . .

Love is what God has given to us; as we give it we fulfil the law (Romans 13^{10}).

This was not accepted easily in the first century, and the man who did battle for it was St Paul. He wrote to the Colossians, 'Why do you live as if you belonged to the world? Why do you submit to regulations, Do not handle, Do not taste, Do not touch . . . ', and to the Romans, 'You are not under law but under grace' (6^{14}).

This battle must be fought in every century.

What conclusions can we draw which will help us to fight it? There are two.

(1) *Everything is lawful which Christian love permits*

'Certainly eat meat offered to idols,' said Paul; 'you and I know an idol is only wood. *But* don't eat if so doing offends the tender conscience of your brother.' All our wishes can be tested here. Do we wish to make money? Do so, but not at the expense of others. Do we wish to eat this, or drink that? It is lawful; but is it wise? are we leading anyone else astray?

'Love God,' said Augustine, 'and then do what you like.'

(2) *Everything is demanded which Christian love requires*

The second part of Luther's book continued: 'The Christian man is the perfectly dutiful servant of all, subject to all.' In the parable of the sheep and the goats, the people represented by the goats had been quite within their rights, within the law, to shut their door and withhold any gift from the poor; but they had failed to obey the law of love. This condemned them.

In 1743 John Wesley issued his *Rules of the United Societies*. He listed the things he expected a Methodist to do and not to do. Was this legalism or Christianity? When we read them in the light of his picture of a Methodist we know the answer. A 'Methodist', says Wesley, 'is one who has the love of God shed abroad in his heart; one who loves the Lord with all his heart, and soul, and mind, and strength. He rejoices evermore, prays without ceasing, . . . and in everything gives thanks. . . . His heart is full of love to all mankind, purified from wrath, every malice and every unkind affection. The desire and design of his life is not to do his own will but the will of Him that sent him.

'He keeps all God's commandments from the least unto the greatest. He follows not the customs of the world, for vice does not lose its nature by becoming fashionable. He fares not sumptuously every day. He cannot lay up treasures on earth, nor can he adorn himself with costly gold and apparel. He cannot speak evil of his neighbour any more than he can lie. He does good unto all men, neighbours, strangers, friends and enemies.'

BOOK LIST

Nature, Design and General Rules of the People Called Methodist (Epworth Press, 3*d*.).
The Christian Character, Wm. Neill (World Books, 2*s*. 6*d*.).
Declarations on Social Questions (Epworth Press).

A FORTNIGHT'S DEVOTIONAL READING FROM THE BIBLE AND 'METHODIST HYMN-BOOK' ON THIS SUBJECT

Day	*Bible*	*MHB*
1	Genesis 28^{10-22}	547
2	Exodus 20^{1-17}	44
3	Leviticus 25^{35-46}	895
4	Deuteronomy 12^{1-12}	385
5	Deuteronomy 26^{1-11}	568
6	Matthew 5^{1-17}	580

7	Matthew 22$^{34-40}$	605
8	Luke 13$^{10-17}$	598
9	John 13$^{1-10, 31-5}$	721
10	Acts 15$^{1-11}$	556
11	Romans 13$^{8-14}$	783
12	1 Corinthians 10^{23}–11^{1}	390
13	Galatians 3$^{1-14}$	434
14	Colossians 2$^{16-23}$	687

QUESTIONS FOR DISCUSSION

(1) Is the Gospel an offer or a demand?

(2) 'Sunday law needs reform.' What would you do about this in the light of Jesus's words,'The Sabbath is made for man and not man for the Sabbath'.

(3) 'Love God and do what you like.' Comment on this word of St Augustine in the light of what we call 'Christian Citizenship'.

PRAYER OF ST JOHN CHRYSOSTOM

O Lord my God, I know that I am not worthy that Thou shouldest come under the roof of the house of my soul, for it is entirely desolate and fallen into ruin, and Thou has not in me a place worthy to lay Thy head. But as Thou didst for our sakes humble Thyself from on high, so do Thou now stoop to the measure of my lowliness. *Amen.*

EIGHT

What is a Protestant?

THE GREAT WORDS 'Protestant' and 'Catholic' have fallen on evil days. Many people today imagine that a Protestant is one who merely exists to protest, and they quote Luther's 'protest' in nailing his ninety-five theses on the Castle Church door at Wittenberg. In 1529, however, the words had a much more positive meaning; at the Diet of Spires, for example, when the Emperor tried to suppress Luther's teaching, a group of laymen, who knew what they believed, made a 'protestation' or 'declared their faith in public'. From this arose Protestantism, by which millions have learned to 'give a reason for the faith' that is in them, so that they could say 'I know in whom I have believed'. On the other hand the word 'Catholic' (which means Universal) is claimed as the sole right of a *part* of the universal Church, the *Roman* Catholic Church. St Ignatius, in A.D. 115, said, 'Where Christ is, there is the Catholic Church', but over a Roman Catholic Church in Manchester stand the words, 'Where Peter is, there is the Church'—Ignatius misquoted: the truth perverted. The Protestant, the Orthodox and the Roman have an equal right to use the word 'catholic', for Jesus said: 'Where two or three are gathered together in my name there am I in the midst of them.'

What does a Protestant believe? He believes the truths set forth in the Apostles' and Nicene Creeds. To make clear how he believes them he would declare three principles reasserted by the Reformers:

(1) *That the Bible is our first and only source of Christian Doctrine*, because it is our first and all-important witness to Christ, to His words, deeds, resurrection and ascension. It is the word of God because it tells us of Jesus, the Word of God. Our Protestant Fathers died for the 'open' Bible, believing that its sense was plain to the man of faith and that one part of the scriptures would interpret another. In practice, the Bible is not easy to interpret, and the difficulty has led to the 'Fragmentation of Protestantism'. Is this too high a price to pay for the free play of God's Spirit in the Church and for deliverance from spiritual totalitarianism?

(2) *Protestants believe that a man is saved by faith alone.* Salvation is God's act of grace and mercy following on our willingness to receive it. Nothing stands between a man and God; the only 'mediator' is Christ. 'If you take away their penances, their relics and their images, these "props" as you call them,' the Roman Legate is reported to have said to Luther, 'what will you put in their place?' 'Only Jesus Christ', Luther replied. This is the clear teaching of the New Testament. The court fool said to a cardinal troubled by Luther's success: 'Take my advice: first depose Paul from the Apostles; it is he who is giving us all this trouble.'

(3) *Protestants believe in the Church: One, Holy, Catholic and Apostolic*, and they make a serious attempt to rediscover the New Testament view of the Church as the Fellowship of the Holy Spirit. This attempt has found expression in two things: (*a*) *Family worship*, with the Family Bible, the family pew and family prayers as its 'means of grace'; and (*b*) '*The Priesthood of all Believers*', where stress is laid on the exercise of spiritual gifts on the part of the laity of the Church, more particularly as preachers and under-pastors of the flock.

In claiming all this for Protestantism we must say a word about the Roman Catholic Church. While recognizing its many great qualities, we cannot admit its claims. A word, in charity, must be said about these. The Roman Catholic Church claims:

(1) *That it is the only true Church.* Jesus, says Rome, gave authority to Peter; he established the Church of Rome, and this 'primacy' is handed down to Peter's successors. '*Tu es Petrus*' describes the Pope. We deny this and say that Matthew 16[17-19] cannot mean what the Romans claim, because (*a*) though it may be true that by 'this rock' Jesus did mean Peter himself (though only seventeen out of eighty-five of the Fathers accept this and the more usual understanding of the saying is that Jesus meant Peter's faith) it could not be understood as establishing an exclusive claim for all time; for only a few days later (Matthew 18[1]) the rest of the disciples ask, 'Who is the greatest in the Kingdom of Heaven?'—a question they could not have asked if the matter had been decided. Peter was the first, after Christ, of 'the living stones' to be built into the Church, and others followed him, for the power 'to bind and loose' given to him was given to all the apostles later (Matthew 18[18]). (*b*) Peter did not found the Church of Rome. It is more likely that it took its root from Pentecost and that Peter was not known there before Paul wrote his letter to the Romans (*c.* A.D.

58), for he does not mention Peter in it and it was not his custom to interfere in any Church founded by another apostle (Romans 15^{20}). (*c*) We do not find the primacy of Peter in the New Testament: it was James, not Peter, who presided over the first Church Council (Acts 15). (*d*) The Roman claim to primacy was not accepted by the great doctors of the Church, or by the other great sees. Antioch, Jerusalem, Alexandria and Constantinople never agreed, and when three of them were knocked out of the argument, the remaining one continued a centre of the Orthodox Church, which does not admit Rome's claim to this day.

(2) *That as the only true Church, it is infallible.* This again is based on Peter's power to 'bind and loose', and only follows if claim (1) is allowed. This second claim does not stand up to history (Popes Virgilius and Honorius were condemned heretics).

(3) *That the Virgin Mary was assumed bodily into Heaven.* This stems from imagination bolstered by infallibility. Not a shred of evidence is to be found for this doctrine; it is created out of popular demand. An Irishman once asked a Protestant open-air speaker: 'Where is our Lady then? Isn't she at the right hand of God?' Peter said that Jesus occupied that position (Acts 2^{33-6}), but the Irishman's words show how much farther imagination could go. We give 'our Lady' full honour as the mother of our Lord.

As Protestants we believe in the real presence of Jesus in Holy Communion in the manner Charles Wesley understood it when he wrote:

We need not now go up to heaven,
To bring the long-sought Saviour down;
Thou art to all already given,
Thou dost e'en now Thy banquet crown:
To every faithful soul appear,
And show Thy real presence here.

We do not believe with the Roman Catholic in 'transubstantiation', by which he means that 'a conversion is made of the whole substance of the bread into the substance of the body of Christ our Lord . . .'. This view we believe to be based on a discredited philosophical theory of the nature of matter, and a mechanical interpretation of the words of Jesus at the Last Supper. He promised to be with His disciples who met in His name, and also said: 'God is a Spirit: and they that worship him must worship in spirit. . . .' We also give due weight to the tradition of the

Church, but do not make it a fetter on the Spirit of God, remembering again the warning of Jesus that it was possible to deny even the law of love by 'your tradition'.

Chesterton claimed that he embraced the Roman Faith 'To get rid of my sins', and the Roman Church certainly offers full cover to any man who accepts its teaching. But faith for a Protestant is not the acceptance of promulgated dogma; it is a personal trust in Christ as Saviour, and here a man stands before God alone and finds Christ to be his companion.

BOOK LIST

Why I am a Protestant, Rupert Davies (Epworth, 7*s.* 6*d.*)
The Faith of a Protestant, Rupert Davies (Epworth, 1*s.*).

A FORTNIGHT'S DEVOTIONAL READING FROM THE BIBLE AND 'METHODIST HYMN-BOOK' ON THIS SUBJECT

Day	*Bible*	*MHB*
1	Romans 1^{16-25}	361
2	Romans 3^{9-39}	381
3	Romans 4^{1-11}	564
4	Romans 5^{1-11}	498
5	Romans 6^{15-23}	495
6	Romans 7^{14-25}	378
7	Romans 8^{1-17}	376
8	Romans 8^{26-39}	370
9	Romans 10^{1-15}	359
10	Romans 12	366
11	Romans 13^{8-14}	372
12	Romans 14^{1-12}	379
13	Romans 15^{1-13}	760
14	Romans 15^{14-20}	478

QUESTIONS FOR DISCUSSION

(1) How far does the hymn 'Rock of Ages' express the faith of modern Protestants?
(2) Has our 'fear' of Roman Catholicism lost us anything (e.g. beauty, drama, colour, order, etc., in worship and Church buildings)?
(3) How can we best rediscover family religion?

A PRAYER OF CALVIN

O Lord God, who hast appointed the night for rest of man as Thou didst create the day in which he may give himself to labour, grant that our bodies may so rest this night that our souls may not cease meanwhile to watch for thee. *Amen.*

NINE

How Methodism Began

METHODISM BEGAN with John Wesley and it will be best to consider his experience. In his day, however, the very word *experience* was suspect: 'An actual experience of redeeming grace was not regarded as a thing to be expected,' wrote Dr Bett; 'there ought to be a moral life and a sincere assent to the Creeds of the Church, and some repentance, since all men have sinned, and there might be some hope of salvation through the mercy of God, if the life had been virtuous enough—and that was all.' John Wesley began by attempting to live this way—that is, by law. He was soon dissatisfied. Returning from America in 1738, he wrote: 'I went to America to convert the Indians; but who shall convert me?' 'The strictest life is but in vain,' sang Luther; and Wesley said of this period of his life: 'I had the faith of a servant though not of a son.'

Soon he had a remarkable experience. In February 1738 he met a German called Peter Böhler. Wesley questioned himself: 'How can you preach to others who have not faith yourself?' And he asked Böhler's advice about it, who answered: 'Preach faith till you have it; and then because you have it, you will preach faith.'

Wesley did this though his 'soul started from the work', and on 27th March he proclaimed this faith to a condemned felon, who kneeled down 'having no rest in his bones by reason of his sins'. Suddenly he got up and said: 'I am now ready to die. I know Christ has taken away my sins.' The following Easter Day, John wrote: 'I see the promise, but it is afar off.' Both John and Charles began to read Luther's works, and on Whitsunday, as Charles lay ill, he heard a voice say: 'In the name of Jesus of Nazareth, rise and believe.' He opened the Bible and read: 'He hath put a new song in my mouth, even a thanksgiving unto our God, many shall see it and fear and put their trust in the Lord.' Two days later he wrote a hymn on his conversion (*MHB* 361). Next day (24th May) John woke at 5 a.m. and read: 'There are given unto us exceeding great and precious promises, even that ye should be partakers of the divine nature.' As he went out he opened his Bible again on the words: 'Thou art not far from the kingdom of God.' In the afternoon at St Paul's the anthem was, 'Out of the depths have I cried unto Thee, O God'. 'In the evening', he wrote, 'I went very unwillingly to a society in Aldersgate Street, where one was reading Luther's preface to the *Epistle to the Romans*. About a quarter before nine, while he was describing the change which God works in the heart through faith in Christ, I felt my heart strangely warmed. I felt I did trust in Christ, Christ alone for salvation; and an assurance was given me that He had taken away *my* sins, even *mine*, and saved *me* from the law of sin and death.' That night the brothers sang Charles's new hymn, and John began to pray for his enemies. Eighteen days later he preached before the University of Oxford on 'Salvation by Faith'—the trumpet call of the Methodist revival.

Out of this grew the 'Methodist' gospel. Wesley once wrote: 'Our main doctrines, which include all the rest, are three: repentance, faith, and holiness. The first we account the porch, the next the door, the third religion itself.' In fact, however, in Wesley's *Forty-four Sermons*, the standards of our doctrine, other 'Methodist Emphases' are to be found as well. These are—

(1) *Free Grace to all.* In an age when men felt themselves condemned without hope or appeal, Wesley knew that if God had forgiven him He could forgive anyone. So he preached that all men could be saved, a doctrine which ran clearly contrary to the eighteenth-century jingle—

We are the sweet selected few,
The rest of you be damned;
There's room enough in hell for you,
We won't have heaven crammed.

To this Wesley opposed his brother's hymn (*MHB* 75)—

The world He suffered to redeem;
For all He hath the atonement made;
For those that will not come to Him
The ransom of His life was paid.

He recorded in his *Journal* for April 1739 that he was 'pressed in spirit to declare that "Christ gave Himself a ransom for all".' He continued to preach this for over fifty years.

(2) *Justification by Faith.* Luther rediscovered this in Paul, and Wesley from Luther. This was the doctrine Wesley opposed to the prevailing legalism of his day. In 1753 Dr Ramsey's principles of religion affirmed: 'The immediate means of reuniting men to God are prayer, mortification and self-denial.' Wesley replied: 'No, the immediate, essential and necessary means of reuniting men to God is living faith, and that alone.' At the end of his life he said the same: 'Fifty years ago I had a clearer view than before of Justification by Faith. . . . I am now on the border of the grave; but by the grace of God, I still witness the same confession.'

(3) *Assurance* was the fruit of faith. Wesley believed it was possible for a man to know his sins were forgiven. In 1745 Edward Greenfield was arrested. 'I asked a little gentleman, at St Just, what objection there was to Edward Greenfield. He said, 'Why the man is well enough in other things; but his impudence the gentlemen cannot bear. Why Sir, he says he knows his sins are forgiven.' Wesley replied to such attacks with the words of the Homily from the Prayer Book: Assurance is 'a confidence a man hath in God, that by the merits of Christ his sins are forgiven, and that he is reconciled to the favour of God.' Such assurance gave the Methodists their characteristic joy.

But the crown of all his teaching was that on *Christian Perfection.* The Methodist Deed of Union in 1932 said: 'In the Providence of God Methodism was raised up to spread Scriptural Holiness through the land by the proclamation of the Evangelical Faith.'

But Wesley's teaching on 'Holiness' was much misunderstood. He gave God all the glory, who alone could perform the miracle and create that 'renewal of the soul in the image of God'. Perfection meant perfect love. Here Wesley joined hands with Aquinas, who said: 'Since love is a participation in the Holy Spirit, infused by God into the human soul, no limit can be assigned to its increase in this life.' Wesley wrote: 'This doctrine is the grand depositum which God has lodged with the people called Methodist; and for the sake of propagating this He appears chiefly to have raised us up.' Such was Methodism in its origin. Truly it has been said: 'Methodism is not a new religion; it is the old religion in earnest.'

BOOK LIST

Books on this are legion, but *John Wesley*, by Cyril J. Davey (Epworth Press, 6*d*.), would give an introduction.

A FORTNIGHT'S DEVOTIONAL READING FROM THE BIBLE AND 'METHODIST HYMN-BOOK' ON THIS SUBJECT

Day	*Bible*	*MHB*
1	Psalm 143	188
2	Isaiah 64	234
3	Amos 5^{18-25}	343
4	Acts 13^{26-41}	371
5	Galatians 2^{11-21}	376
6	Romans 8^{12-17}	723
7	Romans 8^{18-25}	411
8	Galatians 4^{1-7}	412
9	Ephesians 1^{1-14}	406
10	1 John 3^{1-12}	407
11	2 Peter 1	545
12	Matthew 5^{43-8}	550
13	Philippians 3^{7-16}	557
14	Colossians 1^{24-8}	558

QUESTIONS FOR DISCUSSION

(1) 'It is results that count.' How would you judge the Church today—by what it believes or what it achieves?

(2) Discuss Christian joy. Do you understand 'the joy of service' or 'the, mystic joys of penitence'? Is an unhappy man a faithless man?

(3) What do you mean by a saint? Is it true that the Church is not despised because it is holy, but because it is not holy enough?

PRAYER

O Jesus, who alone among the sons of men didst offer a perfect sacrifice of obedience, bend by Thy great love our proud and stubborn wills to Thy will, that we may at last be made like Thee and be acceptable in God's holy sight. *Amen.*

TEN

Methodism's Springboard

FROM THE springboard of 'repentance, faith, and holiness' Methodism leaped into all the world. About 200 years ago (January 1758) John Wesley preached to a congregation in Wandsworth in which were two negroes. Afterwards he asked: 'Shall not our Lord, in due time, have these Heathen also "for His inheritance"?' The answer was *Yes*, for Methodism began to spread, like the plague, 'from house to house'. Finding the churches shut to him and the respectable congregations deaf, Wesley went to the unchurched multitudes of miners at Kingswood and 'submitted to be more vile and preached in the highway'. The growing populations of workers in the great industrial cities of the North heard him gladly, and soon, despite opposition in places like Wednesbury, classes were meeting. The first Methodist Chapel was opened in Bristol in May 1739, and by 1784 there were 358 more. Soon the 'plague' spread to Scotland; to Wales, where in 1735 Howell Harris had prepared the way, 'tearing all before him like a large harrow'; to Ireland; and then over the sea to the far places of God's dominion. In all this, as from the day of Pentecost, it was for the most part the lay pioneer, and not the official missionary, who broke the new ground. Men became Methodists and took the gospel with them to their labours in the far corners of the earth. It was in this way that Methodism reached Antigua, when Nathaniel Gilbert, whose two slaves had heard John Wesley in Wandsworth in 1758, returned there in 1760 and began to preach to all who would hear him. On Christmas Day 1752 Philip Embury was converted and, arriving in New York in 1766, was constrained to preach the first sermon there. Methodist soldiers preached to their comrades, Methodist laymen to their servants and households; the word did 'swiftly run' and soon it won 'its widening way'.

It was many years before official Overseas Missions were organized. They began in the heart of one man. Dr Thomas Coke had been driven out of his church at South Petherton because he preached with too much enthusiasm. He rode to Bristol where Wesley was and asked: 'What shall I do now?' Wesley replied: 'Why, go and preach the Gospel to all the world.' That reply bore fruit, but it was some time before Wesley allowed the seed to be watered. He employed Dr Coke on many enterprises at home, though in 1783 Coke had issued a 'Plan of the Society for the establishment of Missions among the Heathen'. A few years more passed, and still Wesley felt that Methodism had enough to occupy it in Britain and America, but in 1786 Coke was blown off his course by a hurricane and landed not in Nova Scotia but Antigua. Here he found work begun by men like Gilbert, and returning home he raised funds to send out three 'missionaries' in 1788. For more than twenty years he fostered and increased the work, until in 1814 he gave his life for it. At the 1813 Conference, though he was sixty-six, he pleaded to be allowed to take a team to India and Ceylon. The Conference could find many reasons for not allowing him to do so, among them the fact that they hadn't any money. Coke spent the night in prayer and next day offered the whole of his personal fortune (£6,000) if he were allowed to go. Conference agreed, and late in the year Coke preached his last sermon in England on the text 'All the ends of the earth shall see the salvation of our God'. Seven young men went with him. On 13th May 1814, he died while still on the way and was buried in the Indian Ocean. But the work he began did not fail, for Methodism was moved by his death and established missionary societies in every district of the Kingdom. By 1834 work was begun in Africa and in 1850 in China. Meanwhile in America, under Francis Asbury, Freeborn Garrettson and the backwoods preachers, a native Methodism had taken vigorous root.

Methodism was not only extending in breadth, it was extending in depth; it had taken deep root in society and was changing society by its influence. This was done not by lulling people into stupidity, but by arousing them to social righteousness; deliverance was given to the captives and them that were bruised were set at liberty. Methodist lay-leaders, who learned to speak and lead in the class meeting, were prime movers in the Friendly Societies, Co-operative Societies, and early Trade Unions. The Durham pitmen of the Primitive Methodist Church formed the mine-workers union in the north, and most people know of the six Dorsetshire labourers who were transported for seven years for forming a union to raise wages from eight shillings a week. What many don't know is that five of those six 'Tolpuddle Martyrs' were Methodists. Methodism produced honest men who were concerned about their neighbours not only as potential members of the congregation but as citizens of the Kingdom of God, and they tried to change society so that God's will might be done 'on earth as it is in heaven'. Wesley was not content like Marx to sit in the British Museum and scribble principles; he fed the hungry, clothed the poor and naked, began adult schools and day schools, and strongly attacked any evil he could lay his hands on. His last letter was to Wilberforce against slavery. It has been said that the British Labour party owes more to Methodism than it does to Marx. 'Repentance, faith and holiness' hold out more hope for the human race than dialectical materialism.

BOOK LIST

The subjects covered here are many and only the publications of the Mission House and Christian citizenship departments could cover them all. *A Charge to Keep* by Dr Frank Baker and *England Before and After Wesley* by Dr J. W. Bready would help much.

A FORTNIGHT'S DEVOTIONAL READING FROM THE BIBLE AND 'METHODIST HYMN-BOOK' ON THIS SUBJECT

Day	*Bible*	*MHB*
1	Isaiah 61	807
2	Jonah 3	812
3	Matthew 10^{1-15}	814
4	Luke 4^{16-30}	263
5	Luke 9^{1-6}	272
6	Acts 5^{33-42}	829
7	Acts 10^{34-48}	813
8	Romans 10^{1-15}	808
9	1 Corinthians 1^{17-25}	802
10	1 Corinthians 9^{13-27}	792
11	2 Corinthians 4	572
12	Colossians 1^{24-9}	574
13	2 Timothy 4	581
14	Philippians 1^{12-21}	584

QUESTIONS FOR DISCUSSION

(1) 'The Labour Party owes more to Methodism than it does to Marx.' Discuss this. What should a Church member do, or a minister say, about politics?

(2) 'The day of the minister Church is over.' Is it true that the

greatest expansion of the Church has always come through the laity? What does this mean today?

(3) 'Charity begins at home.' Do you see anything wrong with 'Foreign Missions'?

A PRAYER OF JOHN WESLEY

Lord, let me not live to be useless.

ELEVEN

Methodism's Distinctive Practices

IN OUR Methodist churches there is no screen to separate the clergy from the laity, the expert from the 'unlearned'. This is because we recognize no distinction of responsibility between the minister and his people in the spreading of the Gospel; every man and woman is called to be an evangelist and our priesthood is that 'of all believers'. Historically in Methodism this has found expression in some of our distinctive practices which arose almost by accident when this doctrine was put into practice. The first thing to come into being was 'the Society'. A group of men and women asked John Wesley to instruct them and pray with them—'Thus arose, without any previous design on either side, what was afterwards called a Society: a very innocent name, and very common in London, for a number of people associating themselves together. . . . There is one condition previously required in those who desire admission into this Society—"a desire to flee from the wrath to come, and to be saved from their sins".'

As numbers grew, John Wesley found it necessary to distinguish those who were in the Society from those who were not, especially in recommending them to other similar groups. He therefore issued each quarter a hand-written *ticket* to all who were in the Society. Every member today in Methodism still receives this class ticket. This word *class* leads us to the first of the two most distinctive expressions of the priestly function of the laity in Methodism.

The Class-Meeting. Canon E. R. Wickham has called this the 'most creative and tested' expression of Christian evangelism in the last 150 years, and defends its use today on theological, missionary, and pastoral grounds. 'There is need', he writes, 'for smaller, warmer, more community-minded expressions of the Christian community than attendance at public worship alone can provide. . . .' This great means of Christian evangelism which was for over a century the driving force of expanding Methodism, and without which Methodism today is gasping for life and breath, began as a by-product. When the New Room was completed in Bristol a debt remained on the building, and Captain Foy suggested that members should be grouped in dozens under leaders who should collect from each weekly a penny towards the debt. Wesley added: 'This is the very thing we wanted. The leaders are the persons who may not only receive the contributions, but also watch over the souls of their brethren.' In a short time the whole Church was organized into a series of classes each in the care of a lay under-shepherd, responsible to the minister, who should train the members in prayer and discipline by meeting them week by week for this purpose. Soon Wesley considered these close-knit groups to be of the true essence of the Church as the New Testament pictured it. By contrast he called the Church of England 'a rope of sand', because of the casual relation of so many of its members to each other and to the life of the Church; and on more than one occasion he deprived Methodists of membership if they refused to meet in class, because 'they hang but on a single thread'.

As in Methodism laymen share in pastoral oversight, so they share in preaching as *Local Preachers*, of which British Methodism has a great army of 25,000 who work in their 'local' circuits to supplement the ministry of Methodism's 4,500 'travelling' preachers. Five out of every seven services in Methodism are taken by laymen each Sunday and it is impossible to over-estimate the influence exerted in this way by a trained and dedicated laity. This ministry also began by chance.

In 1739 Thomas Maxfield was converted, and desiring to help John Wesley he was left in charge, a few months later, of the Society at the Foundery, while John was in Bristol. He was permitted to pray and expound passages of scripture, but not to preach. Maxfield found it difficult to draw this distinction and was soon preaching with great power. John heard of this irregularity and rode back to end it. He was met by his mother, who said: 'You cannot suspect me of favouring readily anything of this kind. But take care what you do with respect to that young man, for he is as truly called of God to preach as you are. Examine what have been the fruits of his preaching and hear him also yourself.' John heard Maxfield and said: 'It is the Lord, let Him do what seemeth Him good.'

Soon a great army of preachers was serving Methodism. Wesley asked each one: 'Do you know God as a pardoning God? Have you the love of God abiding in you? Do you desire and seek nothing but God?' And he advised, 'Invite, convince, offer Christ, build up. . . . Do this in some measure in every sermon', and added: 'It is not your business to preach so many times, and to take care of this or that society; but to save as many souls as you can. . . .' This advice, originally given to Wesley's travelling preachers, is still the guide today of every Methodist Local Preacher —be he Member of Parliament, Professor, Trade Union Leader or Farm Labourer. Whoever he is, he (and 10,000 others like him) will set off on Sunday morning to take his appointment, backed by a thorough training and with God's word open before him. Without him Methodism would cease to be.

As the local preacher labours in his own area, doing his normal work by day and preaching in his leisure time, so the 'travelling' preacher still moves on from place to place. Two hundred years ago the area of which he was the 'circuit rider' might have been as big as Lancashire and Yorkshire, and he and his beast covered it as best they could. He met the classes each night, preached in the morning and moved on each day. As Methodism grew, circuits covered smaller areas, and today there may be ten or twenty in one city. The preacher, though his travelling within the circuit may be less today, still 'travels' from circuit to circuit as he fulfils his ministry. The itinerancy is hallowed by use and experience, for 'no one ever has *all* the talents which are needful for beginning, continuing and perfecting the work of grace in a whole congregation'.

BOOK LIST

Material on the history of class-meetings and local preaching will be found in any Methodist history, but those who would know the position today will find most help from the Local Preachers Department of our Church.

A FORTNIGHT'S DEVOTIONAL READING FROM THE BIBLE AND 'METHODIST HYMN-BOOK' ON THIS SUBJECT

Day	*Bible*	*MHB*
1	Acts 2^{1-4}	98
2	Acts 2^{37-47}	867
3	Acts 5^{33-45}	873
4	Acts 11^{1-18}	970
5	Acts 12^{1-17}	874
6	Acts 18^{1-11}	875
7	Acts 20^{7-21}	876

8	Acts 21^{7-14}	877
9	Romans 16^{1-16}	251
10	1 Corinthians 16^{15-24}	311
11	1 Timothy 5^{9-16}	323
12	2 John	426
13	1 Corinthians 1^{20-31}	603
14	Acts 6^{1-10}	698

QUESTIONS FOR DISCUSSION

(1) 'Lord, teach us to pray.' Can there be a revival till Christians learn to pray in private and public? Discuss ways, means, and problems.

(2) What lay leadership is there in Methodism, and in your local Church? Is it spiritual leadership? Discuss ways of making it so.

(3) The marks of Methodism were: the class-meeting; belief in justification by faith, free grace for all, assurance and the possibility of Christian perfection; the use of the hymn-book, lay leadership, itinerancy. What are the marks today?

PRAYER OF ST IGNATIUS

Teach us good Lord to serve Thee as Thou deservest, to give and not to count the cost, to fight and not to heed the wounds, to labour and not to ask for any reward save that of knowing that we do Thy will. *Amen.*

TWELVE

Methodist Worship

METHODIST WORSHIP—at once simple and dignified, free and yet not without form—can be the best and worst in the world. At its worst it becomes nothing but a 'hymn sandwich'; but at its best it can shake the gates of Hell. Dr R. F. Horton of Oxford recalled two services taken in a village chapel by the local carpenter: 'His voice was untunable and his diction that of the street. But we were at once brought into an atmosphere of reality. . . . He taught me a two-fold lesson, that effective preaching must have practical points of contact with the lives of the hearers, and must be wrought out in the life of the preacher.'

The voice of experience can be the voice of God, and that voice is the authentic voice of Methodist worship. The Methodist preacher is also free, in leading worship, to draw on all the riches of liturgy and ritual; he is bound only by his own understanding and sometimes by the prejudice and conservatism of his congregation. The Methodist *Book of Offices* contains forms of prayer for all Church occasions and the Collects and the Order of Morning Prayer drawn from the Book of Common Prayer. Our worship as we know it today, with its fervent singing and preaching, was originally a supplement to the ritual of the Church of England in which John and Charles Wesley and their followers continued as long as they were able. When Methodists had to leave the Church of England they took the Prayer Book with them.

Some people are surprised that Methodists today do not feel the need, except occasionally, for formal orders of liturgical worship. 'Why don't you recite the Creed more often?' we are asked. The answer is found in one supreme gift given to Methodism (for the whole Church) by God.

The Methodist Hymn-book. This today contains hymns from many sources, but its foundation is 250 hymns written by Charles Wesley. It is based on a great little book of 525 hymns published in 1780 (the preface of which is in the front of our present hymn-book and should be read). Of this 1780 book, Bernard Manning, a Congregational layman, said to Methodists: 'You talk much and rightly of the work Methodism does for the world and for the Universal Church; but your greatest—incomparably your greatest—contribution to the common heritage of Christendom is in Wesley's hymns. . . . This little book . . . ranks in Christian literature with the Psalms, the Book of Common Prayer, the Canon of the Mass. In its own way, it is perfect, unapproachable, elemental in its perfection. You cannot alter it except to mar it; it is a work of supreme devotional art by a religious genius.' And he added: 'This is your vineyard: do not come one day saying, "Whatever I have done elsewhere mine own vineyard I have not kept". In Wesley's hymns, not divorced from the great tunes of the Handel tradition, you have what only you understand and what (I sometimes fear) you no longer feel it worth while to understand.'

Charles Wesley wrote about 7,000 hymns, many of which are, as his preaching was said to be, 'all thunder and lightning'. They are also a tissue of biblical exposition and theology made singable. We sing the Creed whenever we sing with Charles Wesley. These hymns flowed from him, from the day of his conversion (when he wrote *MHB* 361) to the day he died. He even wrote on horse-back in shorthand and would frequently rush in from a journey crying, 'Pen and ink, pen and ink'. He died on 29th March 1788 leaving his swan song:

In age and feebleness extreme,
Who shall a helpless worm redeem?
Jesus! my only hope Thou art,
Strength of my failing flesh and heart;
O could I catch one smile from Thee,
And drop into eternity!

As John travelled home to his brother's memorial service, he preached in Bolton and gave out his brother's greatest hymn, 'Wrestling Jacob' (*MHB* 339). It was the record of their spiritual pilgrimage; and as the congregation sang,

My company before is gone
And I am left alone with Thee,

John covered his face with his hands and wept. Today, whenever these hymns are sung and, as John Wesley advised, 'lustily and with a good courage', they enrich Methodist worship so that it is second to none.

Other forms of worship, once peculiarly Methodist, are sometimes shared by other branches of the Christian Church. In 1755 the first *Covenant Service* was held in the French Church at Spitalfields, where 1,900 people recited the words of 'that blessed man Richard Alleine'. Since 1782 it has been the custom for Methodists to begin the New Year with this Covenant, saying to God: 'I am no longer my own, but Thine.' A few days before the Covenant Service, on the last night of the old year, a *Watchnight* service is usually held leading up to midnight, when the congregation can sing:

> *Come let us anew*
> *Our journey pursue;*
> *Roll round with the year*
> *And never stand still Till the Master appear.*

Originally, watching through the night in prayer and praise was begun by the Kingswood miners as an antidote to their pre-conversion practice of spending the night in the ale-house where they had 'loudly sung the drunkards' songs'.

Open-air worship (and argument) is still a feature of Methodist worship in some places; and meetings for *Prayer* have been a source of power and are being revived today. *Love-feasts* are almost a thing of the past, but the warm-hearted fellowship of which they were an expression continues as a distinctive mark of Methodist life and worship. Such fellowship is expressed in a thousand ways, but perhaps most movingly at the opening of Conference when the representatives of the family of Methodism sing together:

> *And are we yet alive*
> *And see each other's face?*
> *Glory and praise to Jesus give*
> *For His redeeming Grace.*

BOOK LIST

The 1780 Preface to the *Hymn-book* (in the front of our present book) and B. Manning's *Hymns of Wesley and Watts* should not be missed, nor should the books of Dr Henry Bett.

A FORTNIGHT'S DEVOTIONAL READING FROM THE BIBLE AND 'METHODIST HYMN-BOOK' ON THIS SUBJECT

Day	*Bible*	*MHB*
1	Psalm 33	1
2	Psalm 40	6
3	Psalm 98	541

4	Psalm 137	542
5	Isaiah 6	540
6	Isaiah 35	539
7	Isaiah 52^{7-12}	536
8	Luke 11^{1-13}	533
9	Luke 12^{35-40}	956
10	1 Corinthians 14^{1-19}	959
11	James 5^{6-14}	960
12	Revelation 5^{6-14}	745
13	Revelation 7^{9-17}	747
14	Revelation 15^{2-8}	749

QUESTIONS FOR DISCUSSION

(1) Discuss the place that silence, liturgy and music should take in Methodist worship. Should Methodism follow 'The Christian Year'?

(2) 'Sir, we would see Jesus,' said early seekers for truth. What do *we* expect, and what do we get in Christian worship?

(3) Do we make mental reservations in reciting the Creeds? If so, what are they?

PRAYER FOR AID AGAINST PERILS

Lighten our darkness, we beseech Thee, O Lord: and by Thy great mercy defend us from all perils and dangers of this night; for the love of Thy only Son, our Saviour, Jesus Christ. *Amen.*

THIRTEEN

The Sacraments

FEW THINGS are more melancholy in the Christian story than our disagreements over the sacraments. They have been misunderstood, often misrepresented, and that which should be the focal point of Christian unity has become the bone of contention in our disunity. Despite all, the Spirit of God has striven in the past, and strives today, to maintain the spiritual conceptions of original Christianity against our human tendency to interpret everything in a gross, literal and mechanical way. How *did* the Early Church view the Lord's Supper and Baptism?

Jesus said: 'Do this in remembrance of me.' In His voice there was sorrow because He had to leave His disciples, but a sorrow which endures for a night, for joy comes in the morning. Many worshippers forget this and even avoid the Holy Communion service thinking it to be a mournful occasion—a memorial for a dead Jesus. It is true that we remember His Cross, but we also remember His Resurrection; the two meet in one holy joy. For the sorrow of that last supper was forgotten in the joy of the meal by the lakeside and in the Upper Room where Jesus ate and drank with His disciples after His Resurrection; and after His Ascension they believed even more that He was with them when they broke the bread remembering Him. They believed that He fulfilled His promise that 'where two or three are gathered together in my name there am I in the midst of them'. This is why the Lord's Supper is also called the Eucharist—or thanksgiving. This is why every revival of joyous faith has been accompanied by a return to the Lord's table. This is why the Rector of Devlin in 1751 said: 'I had at sacrament fifty whose faces I had scarce seen at the Church before. . . . They had been very profligate men. . . nine out of ten of them were Methodists.'

God had touched their hearts with joy and they came to meet Him at His table. In coming they did not forget the price of their joy, and they confessed the sin in themselves which sent Jesus to the Cross. At His table they found the new covenant, not written on stone or ratified with the blood of a lamb, but written on their hearts and sealed with the blood of the 'Lamb of God that taketh away the sin of the world'. So they took the bread and the wine; they knew them to be the effective means by which Christ gave Himself to them. Today we too 'proclaim the Lord's death till he come', knowing even as we proclaim it His 'real presence', and at the end of the service we rejoice with the whole Church of God: 'Glory be to God on high and on earth peace.'

It is impossible in a few words to say all that this means to Christians. Whole libraries have failed to reveal it and still men try. This is as it should be, for if Christ is present He Himself will lead the trusting and obedient worshipper into more truth. As members of the Reformed Church, we set our face, however, against the Roman doctrine of 'transubstantiation', a 'miracle' by which Rome believes the bread and wine become the very body and blood of Christ 'handled by the hand of the priest, and broken and ground by the teeth of the faithful' (Cardinal Gumbert, *c.* 1059). This view ('gross, literal and mechanical') makes a 'God of bread that might be devoured by any bold and puissant mouse', as said John Knox. We reject this superstition where the faithful—

> *. . . hear the blessed mutter of the mass,*
> *And see God made and eaten all day long.*

'God is a Spirit, and they that worship him must worship in spirit and in truth.'

Holy Baptism also shows the Death and Resurrection of Jesus. As the New Testament convert was baptized in running river water he left his old clothes on the bank. He went down as Christ went to His death; coming out again (as Christ rose) he put on new clothes. So he 'put off the old man . . . and put on Christ'—Cross and Resurrection together.

But why do we baptize *children?* The New Testament, some argue, only tells of adult baptisms, which must mean (they continue) that no one should be baptized till he can make the act a declaration of faith. We answer: It is true that all first-generation Christians are baptized as adults (even today) because they are already adults when they hear the Gospel; but what are we to do with their children? The early Christians baptized whole households, including, presumably, children; Christ said 'suffer little children to come unto me', and Cullmann argues that the absence in the New Testament of any baptisms of second generation Christians *as adults* might presume that they had already been baptized as children. However, we believe that from the first the children of Christian parents were baptized as children.

This view is strengthened when we ask what happens in baptism. In the *first* place *God acts:* 'He engrafts us into His body.' To say that God cannot do this unless the child can understand it is absurd; the human father says, 'This is my child,' and so does the heavenly Father. *Secondly, men and women act*—father, mother, minister and congregation . . . and we remember that the paralysed man let down from the roof-top was healed when Jesus saw the faith of the four men who carried him, like a new-born baby. *Lastly, the child acts*, not at once, or at first in an adult way; but as a little child learns by slow degrees to love and trust his human father, so he learns to love and trust his heavenly Father; and God does not reject him because his ways are infant ways any more than we do. As Hooker said: 'The habit of faith which afterwards doth come with the years is but a further building up of the same edifice, the first foundation whereof was laid by the sacrament of Baptism.'

BOOK LIST

There is much literature on this subject, the following may prove provocative—

Receive This Child, E. Southcott (Mowbray, 3*s.* 6*d.*).
Early Christian Worship, O. Cullman (SCM, 8*s.*).

A FORTNIGHT'S DEVOTIONAL READING FROM THE BIBLE AND 'METHODIST HYMN-BOOK' ON THIS SUBJECT

Day	*Bible*	*MHB*
1	Mark 1:1–11	751
2	Galatians 3:23–4:7	752
3	1 Corinthians 12:12–13:13	753
4	Romans 6:1–11	754
5	Acts 2:37–42	755
6	Acts 8:26–40	866
7	Acts 16:19–34	865
8	1 Corinthians 11:17–34	757
9	Mark 14:17–26	761
10	Matthew 26:17–30	764
11	Luke 22:14–23	766
12	1 Corinthians 10:14–22	767
13	Acts 20:7–12	771
14	John 6	182

QUESTIONS FOR DISCUSSION

(1) In many Methodist Churches only 25 per cent of the members ever come to the Lord's Table. Why?

(2) 'Most baptisms, like most marriages, might be performed by the witch-doctor; they are mere superstition.' Is this true, and what is to be done about it?

(3) Holy Communion, Sacrament (or 'Oath'), Supper (i.e. family meal), Eucharist ('thanksgiving'), Mass ('a sending out')—what light do the meanings of these words throw on the meaning of the service?

PRAYER FROM THE DIDACHE

As this bread that is broken was scattered upon the mountains and gathered together, and became one, so let Thy Church be gathered together from the ends of the earth into Thy kingdom. *Amen.*

FOURTEEN

Methodist Organization

THERE ARE those who say that the constitution of Methodism is like the British Constitution, and we should 'venerate where we are not able presently to comprehend'. There are others who consider it to be a bureaucratic octopus strangling the life out of the Church. The truth lies between these two extremes, for Methodism's constitution, when it is used in spirit, and not just in letter, gives democracy without mob rule and freedom without licence.

It begins where it should with the rights, duties, privileges and responsibilities of the individual *member:* 'All persons are welcomed into membership of the Methodist Church who sincerely desire to be saved from their sins through faith in the Lord Jesus Christ and evidence the same in life and conduct, and who seek to have fellowship with Christ Himself and His people. . . .'

So reads the statement about membership on the back of the *class-ticket*, and it goes on to urge members to adhere to their privileges and duties by attendance at Holy Communion and the weekly class-meeting, and by taking part in the maintenance of the Church and offering Christian service. The word '*class*' reminds us that every member is gathered, with about a dozen others, under the spiritual leadership of a *class leader* whose responsibility it is to concern himself with the welfare and growth in the things of God of those in his care. The classes, which in their close-knit warm fellowship were in the early days of Methodism the growing points of the Church where beginners were taught and everyone was encouraged, have fallen into disuse in many places today. The Anglicans, wiser than we, are reviving them as the ideal means of dealing with men of our age who are without community and without God. Such a revival in Methodism today would be the biggest step forward we could take. The class leaders form with the minister the main part of the governing body of the Society, *the leader's meeting*. With them every quarter meet others who are leaders in other ways: society stewards, poor stewards, the Sunday-school superintendent, local preachers, etc.

To their number are added representatives elected every year by the *society meeting*. These all meet at least once a quarter and are responsible for the spiritual condition and care of the whole Church.

Within each local Church there is also a legal body responsible for the maintenance and care of the fabric of the church, *the trustees*. It is their task to see that the premises are used well, heated, lighted and cleaned, and that sound doctrine is preached from the pulpit. As a legal body they are not elected annually, but 'the trust is renewed' whenever their number falls so low that they can no longer do their work. The officer who 'goes between' the trust and the Church is the *chapel steward*.

It will be seen that the place of laymen in Methodism is decisive and in some ways unique. Here is the 'priesthood of all believers' in action, for they are not only in charge of the business and administration of the Church, they are given the task of 'under shepherds of the flock' and carry that responsibility to the highest courts of the Church. Each group of Churches is called a *Circuit*, the name deriving from the round or circuit ridden by Wesley's horsemen in the early days. The circuit leaders meet once a quarter, and they appoint the pastoral oversight of the ministers, take responsibility for new developments, co-ordinate the united efforts of all the circuit Churches, send representatives to *Synod* and receive from the Synod the decisions of the *Conference*.

In British Methodism, circuits are grouped into thirty-four *Districts*, and in each of these, Synods meet in May to deal with District affairs and send representatives to *Conference*. They also meet in September to put into action the decisions made by Conference. Conference meets in July and is a democratic body composed of an equal number of ministers and laymen, the great majority of whom are elected by the Synods. Conference speaks for the Church and legislates for it in all things. Like Synod, Conference meets in two sessions: the representative session where all public matters are dealt with, and the ministerial session which deals with the choice, fidelity and discipline of the Ministry. When Conference is not sitting, a number of committees carry on its work until the next Conference meets.

The Ministry of Methodism serves its apprenticeship in close touch with the laity. Before he offers for the ordained Ministry, every candidate must be a local preacher. He must have taken the prescribed examinations in Christian doctrine, biblical studies and sermon preparation, and been subject to the discipline and guidance of the lay and ministerial preachers of the circuit. He must give an account of his conversion and call to preach, and have gifts which fit him for the Ministry. When he offers himself, the Local Preachers Meeting and the Quarterly Meeting must approve of him, and the sermon he preaches is heard by their representatives. After this he takes further examinations and preaches twice more before different groups. At last he comes before the Synod ministerial session, and if his call is then confirmed he appears before the 'July' committee. This committee of ministers and laymen enquires fully into the whole of his previous record, interviews him and decides whether to pass his name on to Conference. If it does so and Conference agrees, the candidate enters college in September. Here he may stay four years, taking the examinations each year and perhaps reading for a degree in the university. At the end of his course, he still continues 'on probation' and works under the close supervision of a superintendent minister, continues to study, takes examinations and preaches for a further two years. If at the end of that time his work is satisfactory, he is ordained. He then normally has before him a journey of forty years.

BOOK LIST

The only authority on this subject is the *Constitutional Practice and Discipline of the Methodist Church*.

A FORTNIGHT'S DEVOTIONAL READING FROM THE BIBLE AND 'METHODIST HYMN-BOOK' ON THIS SUBJECT

Day	*Bible*	*MHB*
1	Matthew 10^{16-25}	778
2	Matthew 11^{25-30}	779
3	John 21^{15-23}	780
4	Acts 6^{1-8}	781
5	Acts 2^{15-26}	784
6	Acts 14^{44-52}	785
7	2 Corinthians 6^{1-10}	786
8	2 Corinthians 4	787
9	Hebrews 11^{32-4}	788
10	Hebrews 12^{1-6}	791
11	John 20^{19-23}	793
12	John 15^{14-30}	481
13	Matthew 25^{14-30}	489
14	Hebrews 4^{9-16}	913

QUESTIONS FOR DISCUSSION

(1) Methodist ministers are called 'travelling preachers': what are the advantages and disadvantages of the system?

(2) Methodism tries to steer a course in its government between autocracy and individualism. Does it succeed? What limits does democracy place on personal preference?

(3) Methodist ministers in training now have a fourth year in college during which they try to get to know the world, and the Methodism, in which they must work. Devise a course for them.

PRAYER

Son of the carpenter, receive
This humble work of mine;
Worth to my meanest labour give,
By joining it to Thine.

FIFTEEN

Methodism's Overseas Mission

WHAT Jan Christian Smuts said of Africa, before he died in 1950, might be said of all the countries of the East where our missionaries are working: 'For better or worse the old Africa is gone and the white races must face the new situation which they have themselves created.'

The world is in the melting-pot and the mould into which it will be poured may well be fashioned in our generation. To the East, Communism offers the economy of 'brotherhood' without the Fatherhood of God which alone makes all men brothers; to the West, while lip service is paid to Christian forms, unchristian ideas guide the lives of the majority of the people. The only hope for the world is that as new nations awake from sleep the universal Christian Church shall be at work infecting new societies with the ever new Gospel of Jesus Christ. In this task our Missionary Society plays a great part.

If we were to write down from our morning paper the names of the places where there is tension or growth (and sometimes trouble), they would, in almost every case, be the places where our Missionary Society is having a great impact. Here are a few: Ghana, Kenya, Central Africa, South India, Sarawak, the Caribbean and Hong Kong. Here the Church advances: 700 new members in Kenya, 400 in Jamaica. This is one of the signs of the times. But time is short, and our 'thin red line' of missionaries is very thin. In Hong Kong, with its 3,000,000 people living in hovels and huge blocks of flats, we have six missionaries, and the Methodist Sunday-school is precariously perched on a roof. In French West Africa one minister may have to care for 200 village churches. At home we have one doctor for about 1,000 people; the same doctor in Africa would look after 50,000 people in an area the size of Yorkshire. What is more, world economics work against us. A cooking-pot which cost 2*d.* in the Belgian Congo in 1938 now costs 3*s.* 6*d.*, and a passage to the West Indies which cost £28 in 1938 now costs £120.

How can the Church meet such a situation? Only by great

generosity and devotion. Between 1955 and 1958 we made a great effort to raise £150,000 of new income towards our budget of £800,000. By the grace of God it was done, and the task is now to continue to do it. This would be a simple matter if the whole Church were as eager as the comparative few on whom the major burden of overseas missionary work falls. But we still hear voices, even today, which say: 'Wouldn't it be better if we converted Britain first? We would say in reply:

(1) *Our Lord commissioned* His Church to 'go into all the world and preach the Gospel'. They obeyed and so do we. Just as a stone thrown into a pond sends out widening ripples, so the Church 'beginning at Jerusalem', went 'unto the uttermost parts of the earth'. Whenever the apostles seemed anxious to settle down, the Holy Spirit stirred them up to fresh activity: 'Separate me Barnabas and Saul'; 'Come over into Macedonia and help us'; . . . and the Acts of the Apostles ends with St Paul established at the heart of the Roman Empire preaching the Gospel, 'no man forbidding him'. We, who take the world as our parish, still accept our Lord's commission and share with every other Church the continuing of the work of our Lord in the hearts of men. Only the very newest Church building has no tablet commemorating past devotion, and no minute book recording past service. We all build on other men's foundations and tread where the saints have trod; and what we have received we freely give.

(2) *Our Lord's compassion* was to all who needed Him, and moves us to a like compassion. Two thirds of the world's people lack bread, a large percentage cannot read, millions are without medicine, and most men live without the hope of eternal life which the Christian Gospel brings. We have all these things, so 'we love because He first loved us'. Here is the greatest reason for missions: Love. A young African once said to the aging parents of a missionary who was returning with him to Africa, 'You must love the Ivory Coast'. He was right; our Lord's compassion calls forth ours.

(3) *If a world Community* is ever to be established which will bring peace, it must be around the Prince of Peace. Russia and China are discredited in the eyes of half the world because of Hungary and Tibet. The West is equally discredited in the eyes of the other half by dropping the first A-Bomb on Japan, and by the fact that the poverty of the East has made no inroads into our standard of living. In such a world the Church of God alone, when it rediscovers its own unity in Christ, can create a world community if it is true to our Lord's proclamation and programme

—'The Spirit of the Lord is upon me, Because He anointed me to preach good tidings to the poor: He hath sent me to proclaim release to the captives, And recovering of sight to the blind, To set at liberty them that are bruised, To proclaim the acceptable year of the Lord'.

In the light of this, everyone who will pray, work and give for missions is contributing to world peace. Methodism gives in two ways. The Women's Work Fund is raised by women for the work of women among women. The General Fund, through direct gifts, missionary boxes and collecting-cards and the devoted work of the Youth Missionary Association and the Junior Missionary Auxiliary, pays for all the rest.

BOOK LIST

See *Kingdom Overseas* (from our Missionary Society, 4*d.*); or *Expanding Frontiers*, Dewy Morgan (Edinburgh House Press, 4*s.* 6*d.*).

A FORTNIGHT'S DEVOTIONAL READING FROM THE BIBLE AND 'METHODIST HYMN-BOOK' ON THIS SUBJECT

Day	*Bible*	*MHB*
1	Acts 1^{6-11}	250
2	Acts 2^{1-17}	267
3	Acts 4^{13-22}	266
4	Acts 5^{33-42}	255
5	Acts 8^{9-24}	599
6	Acts 8^{26-40}	794
7	Acts 11^{19-26}	796
8	Acts 12^{24}–13^{4}	799
9	Acts 16^{1-10}	800
10	Acts 18^{1-11}	806
11	Acts 18^{24-8}	809
12	Acts 25^{7-12}	810
13	Acts 26^{24-32}	811
14	Acts 28^{23-31}	815

QUESTIONS FOR DISCUSSION

(1) In a world Church is the title 'Overseas Missions' out of date? and would it be a good thing if every minister had to spend a term abroad during his ministry?

(2) Have we any right to take Christianity into Buddhist Burma, and is it the same thing as taking Protestantism into Roman

Catholic Italy? Sort out the distinction, and the reason for missions.

(3) 'At last we are free to be ourselves', say many of the Christian leaders of China today. How, and in what condition, should missionary societies cease to work?

(4) 'A Church which ceases to be missionary ceases to be a Church.' Is this true, and does it apply to the individual Christian?

PRAYER

Expand Thy wings, celestial Dove,
Brood o'er our nature's night;
On our disordered spirits move,
And let there now be light.

SIXTEEN

Methodist Home Missions

WHATEVER may be happening in other parts of the world, there are times when the work at home 'seems hard and dry'. Dr Sangster wrote: 'Britain is in Spiritual need; dire and deep need. Our overcrowded prisons, juvenile crime, divorce statistics, a lack of a sense of high destiny, the couldn't-care-less attitude . . . all point one way. Our people are adrift. They don't know what life is for. Existence itself is without meaning for the multitude of them. They have no standards. They half suspect that we may all be "blown up" before long and the only thing to do in the bit of time that remains is to take what you want and enjoy it.'

If our people are to be saved from hearing the words 'Thou fool', the Church must remind them that they have souls to save. These are the 'signs of the times' for the Church; but what are the signs of the times *in* the Church? How do we measure up to the task? In very many places the Church measures up well; but in many more her work is hampered, and the fault is often ours. What does the Spirit ask of the Churches?

(*a*) Almost every year since the war Methodism has lost 1,000 or 2,000 members. This is not because we don't make sufficient *new* ones (these number about 25,000 every year) but because in our moving population many do not arrive in a new area as worshippers, or are not found by the local Church. Can this continue?

(*b*) Despite devoted work, Methodism still loses six out of seven of its Sunday-school scholars. One thousand leave us every week. Is this because the job of caring for the Church's children is left exclusively to the Sunday-school staff?

(*c*) Methodism still has too many buildings and too little spiritual leadership. Is this because we have put our strength into preserving bricks and mortar, forgetting that the Church consists of people?

Could we answer these questions put to us by the Spirit of God, could we heed the call to prayer issued by the Home Mission Department in the name of God, our 'mission' would prosper.

Two other questions, however, demand the consideration of every member:

(1) *How can the organization of the Church best be mobilized* to meet the needs of today? Home Missions have a fine record of seizing opportunities when they present themselves. Out of such opportunism has grown the present pattern of our work. Our *Central Missions* supplemented the normal pattern of Church life forty to seventy years ago when masses of the working classes were untouched by the suburban Churches to which many of the Church's leaders were moving. They still provide in many places a vigorous Methodist heart to a city—but what is their place in the even more swiftly moving and spreading communities of today? *Cliff College* was founded to train the lay evangelist. This is still a vital task, but does its conservative tradition need modification in the light of the wider needs of today and the light which God is 'still making to break forth from His Word'? *Chaplains* are at work in the prisons of our land, in hospitals and in the Forces. The development of Wesley Houses in the great centres where our troops congregate overseas has provided many a Methodist boy with a home-from-home. In our universities, the chaplains have seen a wonderful growth of Methodist Societies in which the leaders of tomorrow are trained today. A more recent development still is the work of industrial chaplains. What further moves should we make into the community? Home Missions were begun one hundred years ago to take the help of the whole Church to difficult places, and this is why outposts of Methodism receive help from this department. The Shetlands are under its care, and in many another lonely place a lay pastor is provided by the Church. Rural Methodism and the coal-fields of our land are receiving special attention.

Where next? New ventures and bold ideas are sponsored by Home Missions: *Film Evangelism* and *Methodist International Houses*. In these ways the organization of the Church has been mobilized. Most of the time Home Missions have been taking the Gospel out from the home into society; but today there is a need to take the Gospel back into the *home*, and there is the opportunity of doing it. *Television* enters an increasing number of homes each week, and our Church is awake to it and is preparing to use it to the best advantage. Equally important is the return to *Home Evangelism* in many circuits. Where people cannot be persuaded to come to church they will often accept an invitation to a home. Canon Wickham recently described Methodism as a 'glorious failure' because she had abandoned the class-meeting. Here is a way to recover it which we are learning from the early Methodists via the present-day Anglican Church. But no 'home mission' is possible without.

(2) *The mobilization of the laymen of the Church.* How can it be done? In their hands lies the future; 'the day of the minister Church is over'. The task of evangelism is no longer the task of the few; it never was. The 'big preacher', the 'great evangelist', always usurped the work of the whole Church, and the shame is that Christians let him take their place. The agent of mission is the whole Church, for it alone can be the body of Christ. Only the whole Church can be in touch with the whole community of the world. To this task *Schools of Evangelism* have recalled the Methodist people; laymen meeting at Westminster and Oxford have encouraged their brethren to take up the task with them, and such unofficial movements as the interdenominational Order of Christian Witness, originating in the mind of a Methodist President, have provided illustrations of how it can be done.

BOOK LIST

Each year the Home Mission Department publishes an illustrated and very attractive *Report* (1*s*.). There could be no better guide to Home Missions.

A FORTNIGHT'S DEVOTIONAL READING FROM THE BIBLE AND 'METHODIST HYMN-BOOK' ON THIS SUBJECT

Day	*Bible*	*MHB*
1	John 15^{9-15}	465
2	Matthew $18^{1-6,\ 10-14}$	592
3	Luke 15^{21-32}	953
4	Mark 6^{30-4}	795
5	John $13^{1-5,\ 12-15}$	797
6	1 John 1^{1-7}	803
7	1 Corinthians 13	804
8	Matthew 6^{19-24}	805
9	Matthew 6^{25-33}	818
10	Luke 14^{16-24}	823
11	Matthew 13^{19-23}	824
12	Luke 12^{16-21}	831
13	John 10^{10-16}	835
14	Luke 10^{30-7}	854

QUESTIONS FOR DISCUSSION

(1) What is it right for a minister to do outside his congregation? Is he a servant of *a* Church or *the* church?

(2) Wesley 'forged a chain of steel, flexible yet each link with its own strength, and the 'glorious failure' of Methodism may not be entirely unrelated to the gradual neglect of his ideas in the palmy days of great congregations'. Discuss our organization, week-night meetings and evangelism in the light of this.

(3) Should our central missions be closed? If not, how should they be kept open?

PRAYER OF BLESSING ON OTHERS

The Lord bless thee and keep thee: the Lord make His face to shine upon thee: the Lord lift up His countenance upon thee, and give thee peace.

SEVENTEEN

Methodism and the World Church

'IN THE providence of God, Methodism was raised up to spread Scriptural Holiness.' This task she continues and 'The field is the world'. How much impact is Methodism making today and what is its relation to other Churches? Of all the world's Christians the Roman Catholics claim nearly half, and the various Protestant Churches (including, the Anglican Communion) and the Orthodox together claim the rest. Protestant and Orthodox are knit together in the World Council of Churches, of which Archbishop William Temple said: 'No human agency has planned this, . . . it is the result of the great missionary enterprises of the last 150 years, . . . it is the great new fact of our era.'

With nearly all the other Churches of Christendom (except the Romans) Methodists met at Amsterdam in 1948 for the first World Council Assembly. Its keyword was '*Oikumene*' (Greek for 'the world') and its symbol a ship, with the Cross as its mainmast. The meeting had long been prepared and prayed for. In 1910 there was a great missionary conference at Edinburgh—the start of the Ecumenical Movement. Faith and Order Conferences, to discuss where we agree and where we differ, were held in 1927 in Lausanne and in 1937 at Edinburgh. 'Life of Work' Conferences to discuss the practical outworkings of our common faith met at Stockholm in 1925 and in Oxford in 1937. In St Giles' Cathedral and St Paul's delegates from 100 denominations and forty countries met, and the Archbishop of Canterbury preached from the text—'Speak to the Children of Israel that they go *forward*'. The war intervened but it only slowed down the coming together of the Churches, and in 1948 the World Council of Churches was formed in Amsterdam. In 1954 the Second Assembly of the World Council met at Evanston, and took as its theme: 'Christ the hope of the world.' Though the Assembly meets only at intervals, its continuing work issues from Geneva, and though we still cannot worship together at the Lord's Table, we are united in reconciliation and healing—most notably among refugees through Inter Church Aid.

What is Methodism's place in all this? She is comparatively small, numbering only about eighteen million members and a community of forty millions, but she is not insignificant: one in every fifty of the world's population is Methodist; one in every eighteen Christians; one in every five Protestants. She has 50,000 ministers, 100,000 local preachers and 100,000 churches. But Methodism has a greater contribution than mere numbers. In the quest for unity, which began when the younger Churches found it impossible to accept the denominations of the mother country, Methodism has given hostages to the future, and in Canada and South India has shared in union schemes. John Wesley said in 1764: 'I have long desired that there might be an open, avowed union between all who preach those fundamental truths, original sin, and justification by faith, producing inward and outward holiness; but all my endeavours have been hitherto ineffectual. God's time is not fully come.' But God's time is coming; and today Christian reunion is the quest of every Christian, because—

(1) *Jesus prayed 'that they might be one'*. Surely we must listen to His prayers. Quarrels within the family were the greatest threat to the infant Church; Paul settled the arguments once and for all: 'I planted, Apollos watered, but God gave the increase.'

(2) *Jesus intended His community to embrace all men.* Men have argued learnedly about whether Christ intended to found a Church, since the word only occurs twice in the Gospels. But He told His followers: 'Go into all the world and preach the gospel,' and 'Lo, I am with you always, even unto the end of the world'. In practice, when they began to do this after Pentecost they found that the Holy Spirit ('the Spirit of Jesus') drove them out farther and farther—to Cyprus, then Asia, then Europe—and drove them out also from their narrow restrictions, so that at first Jewish proselytes, and then even Gentiles were included in the Christian family. As Peter said in astonishment: 'Can any man forbid water, that these should be baptized, which have received the Holy Ghost as well as we?'

(3) *Disunity hinders the progress of the Gospel.* 'Christian killeth Christian in a narrow, dusty room', wrote Chesterton; and the room was the room of the mind. There are still villages in England where two Methodist congregations meet in separate buildings (over twenty years after Methodist Union) and overhear each other sing. 'And the tragedy is,' said one onlooker,

'that we are beginning to laugh at them.' If they laugh at them, they laugh at our Lord.

For such reasons Methodism has felt compelled to discuss Christian unity with others, especially with her Anglican neighbours. In 1946 the Archbishop of Canterbury preached a now famous sermon before the University of Cambridge in which he proposed that the Free Churches should 'take episcopacy into their systems', so that the next step might be intercommunion based on a mutually recognized ministry. In 1955 the Methodist Conference agreed to hold conversations with the Anglicans under the following provisions: (*a*) that the departure of Methodism from the Church of England be recognized as a split *within* the Church of God, rather than *from* it, (*b*) that Methodism has the same liberty to interpret episcopacy as already exists within Anglicanism, and (*c*) that closer relations with Anglicans should not impair our relations with non-episcopal Churches. The Anglicans accepted these with few reservations, and the conversations continue. No definite proposals for action are yet before us, except that we are strongly urged to get to know each other as well as possible.

The chief scandal of our disunity is our inability to meet at the Lord's Table; for while as Methodists we have an 'open' communion table and welcome all who love and serve our Lord in His Church, the Anglican Church regards Holy Communion as an expression, not a means, of unity, and considers that the absence of a united ministry makes it impossible, as yet, for us to take the Holy Communion together. Anglicans, therefore, urge the necessity of the 'Historic Episcopate', though they vary in their interpretations of this. Some see it as being in direct succession from the apostles, handed on, as it were 'from father to son', in the form of the special grace and power given to the first apostles by Jesus. They believe that God's grace can only be given through a bishop and that episcopacy is of the 'essence' of the Church for all time. We find it hard to see this in the New Testament, where the original apostleship seems to have been unique and untransferrable, and where the qualification for apostleship was that the apostle had received his commission from Jesus himself. This is why St Paul found it hard in some places to establish his claim to be an apostle, and why he wrote to Corinth: 'Am not I an apostle? . . . Have not I seen Jesus Christ our Lord?' If this is true, such a qualification could not be handed on.

Many Anglicans, however, have a much milder view of episcopacy; they regard it, not as absolutely necessary for the existence of the Church, but as a gift which the Anglican Church holds in trust for the whole Church of Christ. The Methodist Deed of Union affirms that there is 'No priesthood differing in kind from that which is common to the Lord's people . . . and no exclusive title to the preaching of the Gospel or the care of souls; . . . the Methodist Church holds the doctrine of the priesthood of all believers'. This New Testament doctrine we must preserve, with the other things committed to our charge, while remaining responsive and obedient to the leading of our Lord, who said to His Father: 'Thy will, not mine, be done.'

BOOK LIST

An *Interim Statement of the Conversations between The Church of England and The Methodist Church* is available from the Epworth Press at 3*s*. 6*d*., and a shorter study-outline of it for about 6*d*.

Anglicans and Methodists Talk Together, a booklet for study and discussion, is published jointly by S.P.C.K. and the Epworth Press at 1*s*. 6*d*.

A FORTNIGHT'S DEVOTIONAL READING FROM THE BIBLE AND 'METHODIST HYMN-BOOK' ON THIS SUBJECT

Day	*Bible*	*MHB*
1	1 Corinthians 4^{1-11}	709
2	1 Corinthians 4^{12-30}	710
3	Ephesians 4^{1-16}	711
4	John 15^{1-16}	712
5	John 17^{1-13}	566
6	John 17^{14-26}	713
7	Mark 10^{35-45}	716
8	Matthew 25^{31-46}	717
9	1 Corinthians 3^{1-15}	718
10	Matthew 16^{13-20}	719
11	Matthew 18^{12-20}	720
12	1 Corinthians 9^{1-12}	748
13	Acts 6^{1-8}	534
14	1 Timothy 4	563

QUESTIONS FOR DISCUSSION

(1) In this day of the 'World Council of Churches', should there be a 'World Methodist Council'; and in this day of the local

'Council of Churches', should the local Free Church Council continue? If so, why?

(2) 'Methodists love a bishop as Americans love the monarchy.' What should we gain and lose by 'taking episcopacy into our system'?

(3) What does the 'priesthood of all believers' mean for Methodists—ideally, and in practice?

PRAYER

'I pray not that Thou shouldest take them out of the world, but that Thou shouldest keep them from the evil one; neither for these only do I pray, but for them also that believe on me through their word; that they may all be one; that the world may believe that Thou didst send me.'

EIGHTEEN

Methodism and Peace

NO CHRISTIAN doubts that war is contrary to the Spirit, teaching and purpose of Jesus. Christian pacifists reject war outright, while non-pacifists, although they consider it in certain circumstances regrettably necessary, look upon it only as the lesser of two evils. This division of opinion is within Christian brotherhood, but the resolution of it grows more urgent and more difficult rather than less so. In 1940 Dr J. H. Oldham wrote, 'If war degenerates into the wilful slaughter of the innocent, Christians must either become pacifists or give up their religion', and the Archbishop of York wrote: 'If we go Nazi and then win, it will be the same for the world as if the Nazis win.' How does the debate stand now?

The Christian pacifist would say that Jesus taught us to show love even to our enemies at all times. He would base this claim not on an isolated text here and there but on the whole New Testament, saying with Augustine: 'No fruit is good that does not grow on the tree of Love.' He would add further that his Lord practised this love in becoming incarnate in this world for us sinners, and in being crucified for us, His enemies. Finally, he would claim that Jesus promised to those who believe on Him the strength to follow Him by taking up this cross, and that the Holy Spirit would be their advocate when they stand before thrones and judgement seats.

The non-pacifist would reply that this is true enough, but for the pacifist to expect men to attain to such an ideal in an imperfect world is a counsel of perfection, and does not take account of 'the exceeding sinfulness of sin'. Sin involves man in conflict, and to ask imperfect man to live by love is to presume that the conflict has been resolved. The ideal of Jesus is not suitable to the world we live in now, but shows how we shall live when all men are Christians. Our present task is to see that justice is done, and this involves judgement; and sometimes the Christian is put into the position that however much he may wish for the ideal—love by all men for all men—he must choose between two much grimmer alternatives—war or tyranny. In such a situation, a Christian who would not fight in his own defence is compelled by his love for his neighbour—wife, child, the helpless and the weak—to take up arms in a just cause. The good done in this way outweighs the evil consequences of war itself. The New Testament, he would claim, does not teach non-resistance, but on the contrary enjoins obedience to the state as ordained of God to be the secular power in the administration of justice.

To this the pacifist responds that pacifism is not 'passive-ism', and is more concerned to create the grounds of peace than mere non-resistance: 'Ought we to resist evil?' asked St Chrysostom; 'Indeed we ought; but not by retaliation. Christ hath commanded us to give up ourselves to suffering wrongfully, for thus shall we prevail over evil. For one fire is not quenched by another fire, but by water.' Nor would the pacifist see any contradiction between love and justice. 'Love', indeed, is the fulfilling of the law. Both justice and mercy were satisfied on the Cross; God's mercy gave both.

At this point the argument is merely begun, but we must ask if there are any special factors today which must be considered here. There are three:

(1) The pacifist claim that 'Love will find a way' cannot be lightly made in view of the immense pressures totalitarianism can bring to bear on the mind of man. Brain-washing, the indoctrination of children, the techniques of *Animal Farm*, show that no vague 'democracy' or milk-and-water love could withstand them. The Cross alone is sufficient.

(2) The dreadful power of thermo-nuclear weapons must make the non-pacifist look again at his argument for a 'just war'. Can such a war be justified if it means race suicide, if it destroys the thing it is supposed to defend? 'Where there is life there is hope'—and life under tyranny may be more hopeful than to 'make a desert and call it peace'.

(3) Both pacifist and non-pacifist must look together at the effect of past and present tests of nuclear devices. We are told there is room for disagreement as to how much radiation human beings can stand, but no one disagrees that we are playing with worse than fire. Leaving aside the immediate effects of nuclear explosions (which made the Marshall Islands uninhabitable for more than twenty months) the whole world is now subjected to a continuous rain of radio-strontium from the upper atmosphere, which settles in the bone and destroys the red corpuscles of the

blood. This will continue for many years and there is no protection against it; moderate estimates suggest that at least 30,000 people will die as a result of past explosions. It is also possible that radiation will cause modification in the genes of parents so that succeeding generations of children will be damaged or malformed. Professor C. A. Coulson writes: 'Death stands at attention, expectant, ready to serve, ready to shear away the people *en masse;* ready, if called on, to pulverize, without hope of repair, what is left of civilization. He awaits only the word of command. He awaits it from a frail bewildered being, long his victim, now—for one occasion only—his master.' Is there no other word we can speak? Yes: the word 'Peace'. Peace is a positive thing; the absence of war does not bring peace, but only by removing the seeds of war can peace take root. War breeds in hunger, disease, prejudice, ignorance and poverty. If the nations of the world can be persuaded to put their money *against* (and not '*on*') these horsemen of the Apocalypse, the future will be different. The Christian considers the fact that two-thirds of the world lack food, that there are 20,000,000 refugees, that fifty-five per cent of the world population can neither read nor write, that there is racial prejudice and colour bar at home and abroad as the seeds of future war. He fights these with all his might and in doing so fights war.

BOOK LIST

A Programme for Peace, Edward Rogers (Epworth, 6*d*.).

Nuclear Knowledge and Christian Responsibility, C. A. Coulson (Epworth, 9*d*.).

Some Problems of the Atomic Age, C. A. Coulson (Epworth, 3*s*. 6*d*.).

The Methodist Youth Department published an excellent pamphlet for men who were called to the forces giving both the pacifist and non-pacifist view.

A FORTNIGHT'S DEVOTIONAL READING FROM THE BIBLE AND 'METHODIST HYMN-BOOK' ON THIS SUBJECT

Day	*Bible*	*MHB*
1	Matthew 5^{43-8}	902
2	Ephesians 4^{1-16}	903
3	Matthew 22^{34-40}	904
4	Romans 12^{17}–13^{10}	901
5	Mark 10^{17-22}	905
6	Luke 7^{40-50}	906

7	Luke 11^{5-13}	907
8	Luke 23^{30-8}	908
9	Luke 10^{25-37}	912
10	Luke 9^{51-6}	253
11	Zechariah 9^{9-10}; Matthew 21^{1-11}	271
12	Mark 8^{27-38}	130
13	Acts 17^{1-9}	129
14	Revelation 13^{1-10}	16

QUESTIONS FOR DISCUSSION

(1) What did Jesus mean by 'resist not evil' and how does St Paul interpret Him? (Read Romans 12^{17} to 13^{10}.)

(2) 'Security is mostly superstition, . . . the fearful are caught as often as the bold. Faith alone defends' (Helen Keller). How can the Christian Church express its 'faith' in these days?

(3) Our world 'depends on what man is, and in equal and greater measure upon what we humans think man is'. What views of man are common today? What have we Christians to say?

PRAYER

O God, in whom all our fathers trusted and were not put to confusion, rid our hearts now of all vain anxieties and paralysing fears. Give us cheerful and buoyant spirits, and peace in doing Thy will; for Christ's sake. *Amen.*

NINETEEN

Love, Marriage and the Family

FOR THE first time in the history of Christendom we have in this generation an opportunity of making clear the Christian view of sex. This is possible because women are (in most countries) emancipated. They are leaving their 'Dolls' Houses' and emerging into a world which is no longer exclusively man-centred. At last the Church can turn its back on some unhappy things in its past. Its fight against pagan licence which gave it a warped view of sex led to the extreme of monasticism, the exaltation of virginity, a narrow puritanism, and the suggestion that sex equals sin; now we can say clearly that God created us male and female and looked upon us and said 'it is good'. We have the chance today to show that our bodies are 'temples of the Holy Ghost' and vehicles of holy joy.

Let us hope the Church will accept this task, for new freedom can bring new beauty. It also brings new responsibility, and the Church must still fight that licence which masquerades as freedom and helps to fill the divorce courts with 26,000 cases a year. It is good that sex should come out from under the stairs, but it is necessary that young people should receive Christian teaching as to what we mean by sex and love. More and more school teachers are finding that mere biological information is less than half the story.

What is Sex? It is one of the means God has given us to express our love for each other, and to converse when words do not go deep enough. By it we share His acts of creation.

What is Love? It is a union which produces, in marriage, out of two separate beings one new creation: 'Therefore shall a man leave his father and mother and cleave unto his wife and the two shall become one flesh.' They say 'Love is blind'; but the opposite is true, for those who love see with the eyes of God the true nature of the one they love. 'Love is the revealing of the thou to one another': 'he' and 'she' we remain to the onlooker; 'I' and 'thou' we are to each other. Such a vision accounts for that grasp of the truth which love brings, which calls out selfless sharing and alone justifies sexual intercourse, which, without the vision, makes marriage prostitution. To the question, 'How can I find the right person?' the answer is: '*Be* the right person.' The basis of emotional and spiritual maturity is the ability to *give* love as well as take it; and those who are thoughtful, kind, considerate, honest, appreciative, attract other mature people to them. Some ask: 'How can I be sure it really is love?' Despite Hollywood, marriage is an achievement rather than an accident. It needs to be worked at. Lovers may begin by sharing only their feelings, but they must share much more if they are to live together for a lifetime. Lovers must work out during the period of engagement the basis of common interest and mutual sharing, and in some things of mutual toleration, which will become the ground plan of their life together.

What is the Christian case for chastity? This is a strange but necessary question. A number of voices say that chastity is outmoded; many of our advertisements are sexually tempting; and man the hunter is liable, where standards are low, to mistake lust for love:

> *Love comforteth like sunshine after rain,*
> *But lust's effect is tempest after sun.*

The Christian is chaste because—

(*a*) He believes that, though God has made us for intercourse, the time for it is within marriage. This is because intercourse changes for ever the relationship between two people. Only in the security of marriage can true love flower; the rest is docks and thistles.

(*b*) Our bodies are 'temples of the Holy Ghost' and we must not desecrate them by selfish actions. To use another person for self-gratification is to degrade that person to the level of 'a thing'.

(*c*) Unchaste relationships inevitably involve furtiveness, shame, guilt and anxiety; and actions which produce such wrong and rather sordid results must themselves be wrong.

(*d*) Though some may say otherwise, there is no absolutely certain way of preventing conception, and the risk of bringing into the world a child who is ashamed of his parents and has no proper home background is one which ought not to be taken.

What of Marriage? We believe that God has created this as a gift for man, and the New Testament uses it as an illustration of the relationship between Christ and His Church. Husbands should love their wives as they love their own bodies (since indeed they have become one flesh) just as Christ loves the Church which is His body. In the same way those who are married should give themselves to each other and endure for each other just as Christ gives Himself to the Church and was willing to endure the Cross for it. It is therefore—

(1) *A Life-long Union*, for just as Christ's union with His Church is permanent, and a man's union with his body is permanent, so marriage is permanent. It depends for its life and continuance on loyalty and continual renewal. Love which is to survive the darkest days must be like that of Jesus: able to make sacrifices. True love will go very far in loyalty, faithfulness and reconciliation even to an unworthy partner. Where, however, divorce occurs, Methodism recognizes that sin must be dealt with by love and forgiveness on the part of the Church and is ready in certain circumstances to receive back into fellowship those who are penitent.

(2) *For Children.* Man and wife become 'one flesh' and this takes visible form in a child. This is not to say that childless marriages are not blessed and fruitful; they are, and often other people's children receive the blessing of them. Nor do we say, with the Roman Catholic Church, that sexual intercourse is only for conception. Intercourse brings children but it also expresses love; and conception control may commend itself to the Christian conscience as the best way to preserve the health of the mother and the happiness of the whole family.

(3) *For Fellowship* 'for the mutual society, help and comfort that the one ought to have of the other'. This requires a deeper than material sharing—a sharing of worship, prayer, God's word and Christian service. This is right, for marriage is

(4) *For God.* The marriage service prayer asks that 'they may so live together in this life that in the world to come they may have life everlasting'.

BOOK LIST

Man and Wife Together, K. G. Greet (Epworth, 4*s*. 6*d*.).
Sex, Love and Marriage, R. Bainton (Fontana, 2*s*. 6*d*.).
Problems of Marriage and Divorce, Archbishop Fisher of Canterbury (S.P.C.K., 1*s*.).

A FORTNIGHT'S DEVOTIONAL READING FROM THE BIBLE AND 'METHODIST HYMN-BOOK' ON THIS SUBJECT

Day	*Bible*	*MHB*
1	Genesis 2^{18-25}	775
2	Ruth 4	776
3	Mark 12^{18-27}	777
4	Mark 10^{1-12}	593
5	Colossians 3^{12-25}	970
6	1 Peter 3^{1-7}	397
7	Ephesians 5^{15-33}	84
8	Titus 2^{1-14}	855
9	1 Corinthians 11^{2-16}	859
10	1 Corinthians 7^{1-17}	860
11	1 Corinthians 7^{25-40}	861
12	Mark 7^{6-13}	138
13	Luke 15^{11-32}	136
14	Mark 10^{23-31}	128

QUESTIONS FOR DISCUSSION

(1) Youth today matures earlier but marries later; in the interval there is 'the beat generation'. How can the Church make adolescence a fruitful time?

(2) 'We agreed that my wife should make all the minor decisions, and I all the major ones. . . . It works. . . . Come to think of it we never have any major decisions to make.' How should young couples work out a shared basis for their marriage?

(3) 'A bad parent is better than no parent.' Is this true? In the light of your conclusion discuss divorce.

PRAYER

O God our Father, who by Thy apostle hast taught us that love is the fulfilling of the law, grant to us Thy servants that, loving one another, we may continue in Thy love to our lives' end. *Amen.*

TWENTY

The Witness of the Methodist as a Citizen

IT USED to be said: 'Many are afraid of God, but more of Mrs Grundy.' Mrs Grundy was the one who said 'No' for the sake of saying 'No' and enjoyed spoiling fun, and sometimes the Christian Church's opposition to social evil has been mistaken for Mrs Grundyism. When, however, the Church says 'No' it is for a different reason, not that she may hold up her hands in pious horror at innocent fun, but rather that she may oppose those things which, however innocent they may appear, are really cancers in society, and so that she may give a positive witness for good in the community. No one lives to himself alone, and what we do and what we think affects others; we *are* 'our brother's keeper'. As John Donne wrote: 'No man is an island. . . . Every man is a piece of the continent. . . . If a clod be washed away by the sea Europe is the less. . . . Any man's death diminishes me. Therefore never send to ask for whom the bell tolls, it tolls for thee.'

Consequently Methodists today do not ask themselves about any line of conduct, 'Can I stand this?' or 'Will it affect me?' but 'How will my participation in this affect others?' St Paul faced this question at Corinth. The meat in the Corinthian butchers' shops was brought from the heathen temple which in its sacrifices acted as a slaughter-house. The question was: Could a Christian eat such meat, which had been offered to idols? 'We know', said many of Paul's congregation, 'that the idol is only wood; what difference does it make to us?' 'True', said St Paul, 'you are strong in faith and it will make no difference to you, but beware lest eating in public you harm the faith of some weaker brother who sees what you eat.' This principle of being concerned for the effect of our actions on the people around us has been since then the guiding principle of Christian citizenship, and by it everything we wish, or are asked, to do can be tested. It is not a negative principle but a positive one; we wish with John Wesley 'to do all the good we can', and we ask ourselves, will this or that course of action forward or hold back that desire?

It has been said jokingly: 'If you say "*Sin*" to an Anglican he thinks of divorce; if you say "*Sin*" to a Methodist he thinks of drink and gambling.' Certainly Methodism makes a strong witness against these two social evils. This is not because we do not witness against others, but because Methodism began among working men and the poor where the evidence of homes broken by drunkenness and gambling was most marked. Sometimes today we are told this is out of date. There are those who say 'one little drink, one little flutter, will do you and me no harm'. This is not the main question; what we have to ask is rather, how does it affect my brother today? Let us look at these two things as illustrations of the principle.

(*a*) *Gambling*. An odd sixpence a week would seem to do no one any harm, but what harm is done yearly to the nation by spending 550 million pounds in unproductive flutters? Even worse, what harm is done to society by the encouragement of the idea that it is possible 'to get rich quick', and without work? All true wealth is the result of someone's toil, and if we, by winning a gamble, live on the small foolishnesses of the many, we are parasites. 'If a clod is washed away Europe is the less'—if we cease to add to the common store, everyone is poorer, including ourselves. Investigations of those who have made big winnings have shown that generally unhappiness has followed their success; they have become idle, they have lost their friends or their self-respect. John Wesley encouraged his followers to be hard-working, industrious people, and they were happy people.

(*b*) *Strong drink*. Here again the important question is not whether any individual could drink a pint of beer and take no harm, but 'How does this affect my brother?' Moderate drinking is as great a villain here as drunkenness. No one intends to be an alcoholic, but one in seven of all people is incapable of resisting alcohol once he or she begins to drink. What if our example started another on a downward path and he could not stop? There are 100,000 chronic alcoholics in Britain and many more on the way; in 1956 convictions for drunkenness of those under twenty-one rose by 22 per cent and the rise continues. Many bright lights have been extinguished by drink. Benny Lynch, one-time world fly-weight champion, 'fought another battle with John Barleycorn and lost'. He died of alcoholic poisoning in 1947 aged 34. A single drink can so affect the reflexes of a driver that he can become a menace on the roads. It has been estimated that alcohol accounts for 1,000 deaths and 50,000 injuries each year on the roads of Britain. 'He who touches filth is defiled.'

Jesus said the first and great commandment was to love the Lord our God with all our heart, mind, soul and strength; and the second was like unto it: to love our neighbour as ourselves. To do this requires that we should consider our neighbour's needs, wishes and weaknesses as much as our own. It means that we should not only refuse ourselves to do those things that may harm him, but that we should take positive action in his defence. Our Church takes such action on behalf of refugees, homeless, those in need of care and protection, and many others, through its Christian citizenship department. It attempts to produce the kind of society in which social reconstruction, industrial peace and the right relation between man and man, and man and woman, can mirror the intention God has for His children 'that they might have life and have it more abundantly'.

BOOK LIST

What does Methodism Say? summarized by Edward Rogers (Epworth Press, 9*d*.).

A FORTNIGHT'S DEVOTIONAL READING FROM THE BIBLE AND 'METHODIST HYMN-BOOK' ON THIS SUBJECT

Day	*Bible*	*MHB*
1	Romans 2^{1-16}	890
2	2 Samuel 12^{1-15}	891
3	Romans 7^{7-25}	894
4	2 Corinthians 5^{11-19}	893
5	Philippians 3^{7-16}	892
6	1 John 2^{12-17}	896
7	Matthew 6^{28-34}	897
8	Mark 12^{28-34}	57
9	Ephesians 6^{10-20}	260
10	1 Corinthians 2^{26-31}	401
11	Matthew 10^{34-42}	578
12	Ephesians 5^{5-21}	872
13	1 Kings 21	922
14	Matthew 5^{27-32}	707

QUESTIONS FOR DISCUSSION

(1) Is conscience unreliable because it seems to vary from land to land, and from age to age?

(2) 'Guidance involves being able to give a reasoned account of the decision we arrive at.' How far do you agree?

(3) Is it right that judgements may differ between Christians? What about Sunday observance? Alcoholic drinks? Monogamy? Gambling? Pacifism? Should we always tell the truth?

PRAYER

Saviour divine, who perpetually for suffering humanity dost bear the burden, the dread, relentless burden of redemption: we pray Thee that we Thy servants today may, with our weak hands, uplift a little corner of the weight which bears on Thee. *Amen.*

TWENTY-ONE

The Modern Methodist faces His Opportunity

ST PAUL, borne down by the troubles of the world and the quarrels of the Church, cried out 'Who is sufficient for these things?' and answered his own question immediately with the words: 'Our sufficiency is of God.' The modern Methodist, faced with both the needs and the temptations of the world, can only say the same. For us, as for St Paul, the Cross, heavy though it is to carry, is the way to life. When Bishop Hannington died in Africa, he said to those who murdered him: 'Tell the king that I open the way to Uganda with my life.' In a far more wonderful way, Christ has by His death opened the way of life to us, and when He calls us to take up our cross and follow Him, it is not a road that leads to death but to life. The way to be free is to serve; the way to live is to die to self. Why is this?

Anything which defeats us when we struggle on alone—our own sin and the sin of the world—is smashed and defeated when we meet it with Christ. 'I live, yet not I, but Christ liveth in me', said St Paul, and just as surely Christ lives today in the Christian who serves Him. So as Christ conquers, we conquer: 'There is no tribunal so magnificent, no throne so stately, no show of triumph so distinguished, no chariot so elevated, as is the gibbet on which Christ has subdued death and the devil and trodden them under his feet.' So wrote Calvin. In Christ's victory we share, and we press on through service and sacrifice to that day when 'we shall be like Him for we shall see Him as He is.'

Until then, in order to meet the constant pressures of the world and be worthy of the love that God bears us, the modern Methodist, like every other Christian, accepts the disciplines and privileges of Christian service as the hard metal of the road on which he walks to God. Three things are part of this discipline.

(1) *Constant attendance at the means of grace, private and corporate Bible-study, and worship.* These have always been the ways of understanding. A Christian belongs to a family. 'The Bible', said John Wesley, 'knows nothing about solitary religion.' Those who claim to be 'nearer God's heart in a garden than anywhere

else on earth' rarely are; it is their excuse for failure in fellowship. Sometimes, when the devil is strong, we need much loyalty and obedience to bring us to the house of God, but when we come Christ never fails us. It is a significant thing that whenever we think of those great movements of God's Spirit which we call revival, and whenever we wish that the pattern could be repeated in our own day, we see that faithful worship, study of the Bible and prayer were the channels by which God's Spirit came. The Early Church 'continued steadfastly in the apostles' teaching and fellowship, in the breaking of bread and the prayers'. Luther prayed and studied—'Bound by my conscience and the word of God'. Wesley's heart was strangely warmed, but it was by the heat of scripture, and as Methodism progressed in the land it was marked by a deeper understanding of the Bible, a great volume of beseeching prayer and multitudes at the Lord's table. We too might pray today:

Come in Thy pleading Spirit down
To us who for Thy coming stay;
Of all Thy gifts we ask but one,
We ask the constant power to pray:
Indulge us, Lord, in this request;
Thou canst not then deny the rest.

(2) *The discipline of witness.* 'Ye shall be my witnesses', said Jesus, and His disciples went out at His bidding from Jerusalem first to Samaria, then to Asia and the islands of the Mediterranean, then to Europe, until at last Paul preached in Rome, 'no man forbidding him.' Everywhere the message was 'We are witnesses', and our message is the same today: 'What we have felt and seen with confidence we tell.' Reason may be our school-master to lead us to Christ, but it is what He has done for us which is our ultimate authority for witnessing. He has brought *us* to repentance and faith, and what He has done for us He can do for others. Too many Christians try to exercise this privilege through others:

In the stress and strain of struggle
On the battlefield of life,
You will mostly find the Christian
Represented by his wife.

True joy does not lie that way; only those who witness know the fullness of Christian assurance.

(3) *The dedication of our gifts and talents*, including our money. Jesus knew that money was dangerous, He knew that it must be tamed, but He did not look upon it as evil. Money is the symbol of our stewardship of life and can be used greatly for God's glory. John Wesley preached a famous sermon on money in which he advised the Methodist people to 'get all you can (so long as you do it honestly), save all you can (by not spending it on yourself), and give all you can'. He practised what he preached. In all our giving to God and His Church we should ask ourselves the right question: not 'What does the Church need?' or 'How much can I spare?', but 'How much do I need to give for my own spiritual good?' There is no command here for the Christian, only the compulsion of love. Jesus said of the woman who poured precious ointment on His feet that because she had been forgiven much, therefore she loved much. The same is true of us.

At last God calls His servants home. A memorial tablet in a church in the Black Country has five texts on it: the life history of a Christian—

He was born of God
He lived by faith
He went about doing good
He died in the Lord
His memory is blessed

What servant could ask for more?

BOOK LIST

The *Westminster Pamphlets* by Dr Sangster (Epworth Press, 6*d*. each), give food for thought on this subject to all serious-minded Methodists.

A FORTNIGHT'S DEVOTIONAL READING FROM THE BIBLE AND 'METHODIST HYMN-BOOK' ON THIS SUBJECT

Day	*Bible*	*MHB*
1	Matthew 6^{19-34}	670
2	Luke 12^{16-21}	675
3	Malachi 3^{8-12}	676
4	2 Timothy 6^{6-12}	680
5	James 2^{1-8}	382
6	Luke 4^{16-24}	383
7	Matthew 6^{5-15}	384

8	Luke 18^{1-14}	386
9	Philippians 3^{7-14}	387
10	2 Timothy 4^{6-8}	388
11	Luke 10^{1-11}	389
12	Mark 6^{7-11}	396
13	Luke 24^{36-48}	399
14	Matthew $28^{9-10,\ 19-20}$	415

QUESTIONS FOR DISCUSSION

(1) Is it enough to say to a man 'Follow Jesus', or ought a Christian to have a simple rule of life worked out for himself? Make your suggestions.

(2) Do you think that Christian behaviour and worship narrow life? If not, why have so many people a horror of 'being good'.

(3) Is the story of the seventy (Luke 10) a story about extra-ordinary people, or is it a pattern for all Christians? What could you do, and not do, for Christ?

PRAYER

Gracious God, who art the giver of every good and perfect gift, teach us how to give. Show us how to open our hands generously in the presence of another's need, and open our mouths to offer them what they need most, even our Lord Jesus Christ. We ask it in His name. *Amen.*